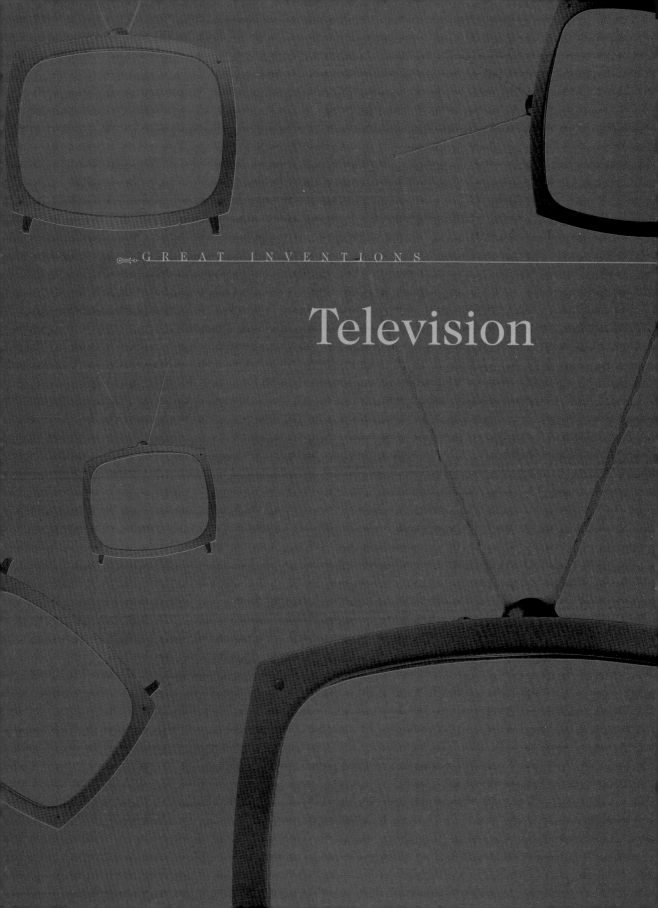

Television

GREAT INVENTIONS

Television

STEVEN OTFINOSKI

Marshall Cavendish
Benchmark
New York

To Mom and Dad, who watched me watching Howdy Doody
in my little chair every afternoon.

Marshall Cavendish Benchmark
99 White Plains Road
Tarrytown, NY 10591-9001
www.marshallcavendish.us

Copyright © 2007 by Marshall Cavendish Corporation

Library of Congress Cataloging-in-Publication Data

Otfinoski, Steven.
Television / by Steven Otfinoski.— 1st ed.
p. cm. — (Great inventions)
Includes bibliographical references and index.
Summary: "An examination of the origin, history, development, and societal
impact of television"—Provided by publisher.
ISBN-13: 978-0-7614-2228-0
ISBN-10: 0-7614-2228-5
1. Television—Juvenile literature. 2. Television—United
States—History—Juvenile literature. I. Title. II. Series: Great
inventions (Marshall Cavendish Benchmark)

TK6630.O84 2006
621.388—dc22

2005026787

Series design by Sonia Chaghatzbanian

Photo research by Candlepants, Inc.

Cover photo: Getty Images

The photographs in this book are used by permission and through the courtesy of: *Getty Images:* Louie Psihoyos, 2; Time & Life Pictures, 31; 79. *Corbis:* G. Schuster/zefa, 8, 92-93; Bettmann, 14, 19, 20, 23, 24, 38, 44, 54, 57, 58, 62, 64, 65, 69, 71; Schenectady Museum/ Hall of Electrical History Foundation, 26, 28; Reuters, 48, 50, 53, 85; Trinette Reed, 60; ER Productions, 73; George B. Diebold, 76; Roger Ball, 80; Lester Lefkowitz, 83; Steve Starr, 87; Yuriko Nakao/Reuters, 90. *Photo Researchers Inc.:* Sheila Terry, 10; Science Picture Library, 11, 16. *The Image Works:* Mary Evans Picture Library, 13; SSPL, 89. *Photofest:* 30, 32, 34, 36, 37, 41, 46, 47.

Printed in China
1 3 5 6 4 2

CONTENTS

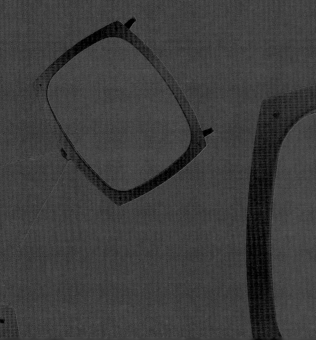

Television

TELEVISION BOMBARDS US WITH THOUSANDS OF IMAGES WEEKLY AND IS A DOMINANT FORCE IN OUR LIVES TODAY.

Beginnings

Unlike the electric light, the washing machine, and the stove, television is not a household necessity. We could live quite well without it. There are even people who pride themselves on not owning a television set or, if they do, never watching it. But they are in an extreme minority.

Few modern inventions dominate our lives as completely as television. While most of us turn on our televisions for entertainment after a long day, television is much more than a conduit for situation comedies (better known as sitcoms), cop shows, and music videos. Television is our primary source for news, weather reports, sports scores, and other information. It is a treasure house of entertainment, reflecting society's broad interests and diverse cultural expressions.

Television is also the ultimate salesperson, bombarding us daily with hundreds of commercials, some of them more entertaining and memorable than the programs they are packaged in. Television is the gathering place for us all in times of triumph (the moon landing of 1969) and times of tragedy (the terrorist attacks of September 11, 2001). For better or worse, television is a powerful medium that shapes our lives in countless, often unnoticeable, ways. Take away television and you take away most people's window on the world.

It is hard for most of us to imagine a time when there was no television. But even devoted baby boomers, the first generation that grew up

SELENIUM WAS ONE OF THREE ELEMENTS DISCOVERED BY SWEDISH CHEMIST JONS JACOB BERZELIUS, WHO ALSO CREATED THE FIRST ACCURATE TABLE OF ATOMIC MASSES FOR TWENTY-EIGHT OF THE ELEMENTS.

watching television, might be surprised to learn that television programs were being broadcast, however experimentally, as early as the late 1920s and that regular programming was reaching those households with television sets as early as 1940.

Television was a dream in the minds of visionary tinkers and inventors long before it became a practical and workable medium. Unlike the electric lightbulb or radio, television was not the invention of one person. Many creative minds went into its creation, which took decades to perfect. Television was not so much invented as it was developed and evolved over time.

A Magical Element

The ability to transmit images through space and then reproduce them on a screen was the stuff of science fiction until a startling discovery was made in 1873. Scientists learned, quite by accident, that selenium, a nonmetallic element discovered in 1817 by Swedish chemist Jons Jacob Berzelius, has the ability to conduct electricity much like a metal when light was shined on it. The light shone on selenium, they further noted, could be transformed into electrical signals. These signals, at least in theory, could then be transmitted and reorganized to reproduce an image.

Perhaps the first pioneer in the long history of television's evolution was an American inventor named G. R. Carey. In 1877 Carey conceived of a kind of mosaic or grouping of selenium cells on which an image could be formed. He proposed that a second mosaic, composed of electric lights, could be set up nearby with each light attached by an individual wire to each selenium cell. An image could then be transferred from the first mosaic to the second, where it could be seen by the human eye.

Carey never built his primitive model due to the impracticality of all those connecting wires. But, crude as it was, his notion of sending and receiving images through two mediums proved to be a basic concept fundamental to the successful transmission of television signals.

Carey and others tried to refine this system by various methods— replacing the multitude of wires with one central one, replacing the selenium mosaic with a single cell, and scanning the image by means of a moving mirror. But none of these worked to any degree of satisfaction.

The Nipkow Disk

The next important figure in the development of television was German inventor Paul Gottlieb Nipkow. In 1884, when he was twenty-four, Nipkow filed a patent for an image-transmitting system that used a simple scanning disk, a great advance over Carey's crude mosaic of cells. The disk was perforated with small holes in a spiral pattern. When spun rapidly, the rotating disk scanned through each hole a line or part of an image that could then be transformed into electrical impulses. These impulses could be

GERMAN INVENTOR PAUL NIPKOW, WHO DIED IN 1940, LIVED TO SEE HIS MECHANICAL SCANNER DISK DISPLACED BY AN ELECTRONIC TELEVISION SYSTEM.

transmitted to an identical receiving disk connected to the first one and moving in a similar motion. The second disk would transform the electrical impulses line by line to reconstruct the image, which could be viewed on a tiny tube in front of the receiving disk.

Nipkow never built a working model of his invention, but others did and named it the "Nipkow Disk" in his honor. This mechanical device became the key for television-like systems for the next fifty years.

The scanning disk proved effective, but from the start it had severe limitations. The image could only be sent over short distances. To get a clear, sharply defined image, bigger and bigger disks needed to be built, making the entire system cumbersome and impractical. A more effective way of sending images through space was a transmitter that used electric or electromagnetic waves. The Italian inventor Guglielmo Marconi had used an electronic transmitter in 1895, when he sent radio signals through the air for the first time. By the turn of the century several lone inventors were trying to find a way to send images through the air as effectively as Marconi had transmitted sound waves.

The Cathode-Ray Tube

In 1897 German physicist K. F. Braun invented the cathode-ray oscilloscope. This glass tube contained electrodes, conductors that emitted cathode rays, an invisible form of radiation, when connected to a source of electrical energy. The rays caused the tube to glow with a bright fluorescence.

Braun did not apply the cathode-ray oscilloscope to the transmission of images, but other scientists eventually did. One of the most prominent of these was Boris Rosing, a professor at the Technological Institute of Saint Petersburg in Russia. In 1902 Rosing began experiments in which he used the cathode-ray tube to receive images. Five years later, he constructed a system that transmitted an image, which was then received by and reproduced on a cathode-ray tube.

Other inventors were developing an electrical system along similar lines, although it was still far from practical. In 1907 the word *televi-*

JOHN LOGIE BAIRD, TELEVISION PIONEER, TELEVISES THE IMAGE OF A VENTRILOQUIST'S DUMMY'S HEAD WITH HIS MECHANICAL TELEVISION SYSTEM. THE HOT LIGHTS NECESSARY TO REPRODUCE AN IMAGE WOULD HAVE BEEN TOO UNBEARABLE FOR A HUMAN TO ENDURE.

sion was used for the first time, in an article in the periodical *Scientific America.* The word was composed of a Greek and a Latin root—*tele,* meaning "far off" and *vision,* meaning "to see."

In 1914 World War I broke out in Europe, and much of the work on further developing television came to a halt. Scientists turned their attention instead to devising new weapons of warfare for their respective nations. Not until the early 1920s would four remarkable men renew the search for a practical television system.

Mechanical versus Electronic

Of the four men who resumed the struggle to make television a working reality, two were Americans, one was Scottish, and the other Russian. Two worked on perfecting the mechanical system based on the Nipkow Disk, while the other two pursued a new electronic system.

John Logie Baird was an engineer and tinker from Helensburgh, Scotland. He later moved to London and then to Hastings where he attempted to create a workable mechanical television system in an attic workshop in 1924. Back in London, on October 2, 1925, Baird made the first transmission of a still and a moving image. The still image was of a face, not a human one, but of a ventriloquist's dummy. Baird used the inanimate object because he had no assistant and humans could not stand prolonged exposure to the extremely hot lights that were necessary to project an image successfully onto his disk. This heat problem would plague developers of television for decades to come.

In January 1926, Baird gave the first public demonstration of his system to members of the Royal Institution of England. They were duly impressed. Two years later he transmitted a picture signal from Kent, England, across the Atlantic to Hartsdale, New York. Baird's great success led the British Broadcasting Corporation (BBC), formerly a radio network, to adopt his television system in 1929. Germany also adopted Baird's system the same year.

At the same time Baird was working in England, American Charles Francis Jenkins was achieving similar results with his mechanical system. Jenkins was in his fifties when he turned his attention to television and was already an accomplished inventor. He had invented the first successful movie projector, the phantascope, in 1894. In 1923 Jenkins transmitted a picture of President Warren G. Harding from Washington, D.C., to Philadelphia, a distance of about 100 miles (161 kilometers).

The mechanical system seemed to be setting the direction for television's future, but those who believed in an electronic system were also hard at work. Back in 1908, English inventor A. A. Campbell Swinton improved on Rosing's system by proposing that cathode-ray tubes be used for both sending and receiving images, making for an all-electronic system.

It took an eighteen-year-old farm boy from Idaho, Philo Farnsworth, to create the first electronic system that would rival Baird and Jenkins's mechanical one. Farnsworth figured out that electrons, negatively

A PROUD TWENTY-TWO-YEAR-OLD PHILO FARNSWORTH POINTS TO HIS INVENTION, THE FIRST ELECTRONIC TELEVISION.

Philo Farnsworth—Boy Wonder of Television

If Philo Farnsworth's contribution to the invention of commercial television has been largely overlooked in the past, it might be because he did not have a corporation behind him financing and promoting his work.

Farnsworth decided at age six that he was going to be an inventor. His first "invention" was using a toy dynamo that generated electrical current to run a tiny motor that would operate his mother's sewing machine. The Farnsworths moved from Idaho to Utah when Philo was twelve. Farnsworth attended Brigham Young University where he amazed his professors with his inventive mind.

After conceiving of his electronic system of television, Farnsworth married and moved to California. He continued his work secretly in a room of the couple's apartment that he converted into a laboratory. Neighbors were suspicious of what he was up to and summoned the police, who thought Farnsworth might be running a bootleg liquor operation out of his home.

When the Radio Corporation of America (RCA) began to manufacture television tubes in the 1930s, they used Farnsworth's system without paying him a royalty. He sued them and won. RCA was forced to give him credit for the tube and pay him a royalty. In 1938 Farnsworth opened his own Farnsworth Television and Radio Corporation in Delaware, but it could not compete with broadcasting giants such as RCA's National Broadcasting Company (NBC). He continued to invent and held more than two hundred patents by the time of his death in 1971.

VLADIMIR ZWORYKIN'S ICONOSCOPE, AN EARLY FORM OF ELECTRICAL SCANNER, WAS NOT APPRECIATED BY HIS EMPLOYER, WESTINGHOUSE. HE LATER DEVELOPED HIS COMPLETE TELEVISION SYSTEM AT CORPORATE RIVAL RCA.

charged particles, when contained inside a vacuum tube, could be set in motion so as to break down an image and convert it into an electronic signal that could then be sent through the air and received and reconstructed elsewhere, line by line.

Farnsworth called his improved cathode-ray tube a "dissector," and he applied for a patent for it in January 1927. Two years later he gave a public demonstration, a transmission of swirling cigarette smoke. In 1930, at the age of twenty-three, Farnsworth filed for a patent for a cathode-ray scanner to receive and reproduce pictures.

Zworykin's Iconoscope and Kinescope

While Farnsworth was laboring in his home laboratory, a Russian émigré was developing the first television camera in the laboratories of an American company. Vladimir Zworykin was one of Professor Rosing's brightest pupils at the Technological Institute in Saint Petersburg. Zworykin left his homeland in 1919 during the Russian Revolution and settled in the United States. The Westinghouse Company hired him to work on television technology in their research laboratories in East Pittsburgh, Pennsylvania. Zworykin's iconoscope consisted of a light-sensitive mosaic and an electronic beam that scanned images line for line. As it scanned, the beam caused an electric charge to be released from each photoelement in the mosaic. The iconoscope freed television from the limitations of the Nipkow Disk. The number of lines in the reconstituted picture had a far greater range and could produce a much sharper picture.

In 1923 Zworykin demonstrated his iconoscope for his bosses at Westinghouse. While they found the invention "extremely interesting," Zworykin later recalled, they suggested that "it might be better if I were to spend my time on something a little more useful." They failed to see the potential of commercial television and did not want to risk spending money on a new system that was still only in the developmental stage.

But Zworykin persevered. By 1929 he had invented a new and better cathode-ray picture tube that could receive the image sent by the iconoscope. He called it the kinescope.

"A Photograph . . . Come to Life"

On August 7, 1927, a mechanical scanner was used to send television signals over telephone lines connecting Washington, D.C., and New York City. The Secretary of Commerce Herbert Hoover viewed the transmission in Washington and declared "it was as if a photograph had suddenly come to life . . ."

The General Electric Company (GE) opened the first experimental television station, WGY, in Schenectady, New York, in 1928. A Schenectady resident became the first home television viewer in May of that year, receiving programs three afternoons each week. It must have been hard for him and his family to see the broadcasts, however, because the screen of the prototype television set was only about 1.5 square inches (9.7 square centimeters) in size.

WGY was responsible for several firsts in 1928. In August it transmitted the first remote broadcast when it televised New York governor Al Smith accepting the Democratic nomination for president in Albany, New York. Smith would lose to Republican Hoover in the fall election.

On September 11, 1928, the station aired the first live play on television, a routine melodrama called *The Queen's Messenger*. Each actor had a camera trained on him or her throughout the broadcast. Those viewing could only see their faces on the small screen. The critic from *The New York Times* was not impressed. "The pictures are about the size of a postal card and are sometimes blurred and confused," he wrote.

Meanwhile, Zworykin was ready to demonstrate his iconoscope and new kinescope for Westinghouse executives. Again, they were less than enthusiastic. But one person who attended the presentation had a very different reaction. David Sarnoff was a vice president and general manager at RCA, who had early on seen the entertainment potential of radio.

DAVID SARNOFF, TELEVISION'S FIRST GREAT ENTREPRENEUR, GOT HIS START IN RADIO. HERE HE IS PASSING THE RADIO CODE PROFICIENCY TEST AT A FORT MONMOUTH, NEW JERSEY, SIGNAL SCHOOL, AS A MEMBER OF THE U.S. ARMY SIGNAL CORPS RESERVES IN 1930.

In 1926 he founded RCA subsidiary the National Broadcasting Company (NBC), which quickly became the biggest radio network in America. When Sarnoff saw Zworykin's demonstration, he witnessed new potential in television, in the wedding of sight and sound. He asked Zworykin what it would cost to perfect his invention. Zworykin reeled off the figure $100,000. Sarnoff replied "it's worth it." Shortly after, Zworykin left Westinghouse and went to work for RCA, not as a lone researcher, but as the head of an entire department dedicated to developing his new electronic system of television. David Sarnoff and RCA were ready to risk everything on electronic television. While it would end up costing them millions, not thousands of dollars, it was a gamble that would pay off handsomely.

An invited audience squeezes in an early television studio in April 1931 to watch the first regular broadcast of a synchronized sight and sound television program at W2XCR in New York City, one of sixteen early experimental television stations that broadcast programming between 1928 and 1939.

The Race for Television

On July 30, 1930, a new era in the history of television began when NBC officially opened its first experimental television station, W2XBS, in New York City. About a year to the day after, the second-largest radio network, the Columbia Broadcasting System (CBS)—initially established in 1927—inaugurated its own television station, W2XAB. CBS boasted that its station would have the first seven-days-a-week broadcasting schedule. This might have sounded impressive, but since there were no commercial television sets yet on the market, the only viewers who could enjoy CBS's daily programming were those who had access to one of their laboratory or public monitor screens.

The two fledgling networks were nonetheless anxious to show the world that television was more than just a passing novelty. In 1932 both stations covered the presidential election results that declared Franklin D. Roosevelt the new president. While Roosevelt would prove himself a master communicator in his famous "fireside chats" on the radio, he would also be, however sporadically, the first president to address the nation on television.

NBC went mobile, taking their cameras out of the studio, to show scenes of the construction of New York City's Rockefeller Center. During the filming, cameramen accidentally caught the first unfolding live news story when a woman fell to her death from the new building's eleventh floor.

The Downfall of Mechanical Television

The Federal Communications Commission (FCC) was formed in 1934 to regulate interstate communications by radio and television. The group recognized television as a promising new medium, but wanted to wait and see how it would develop before granting it full commercial status. As a result, the FCC refused to issue commercial television licenses until it felt the new medium had fully proved itself. Broadcasters, mostly those who operated radio stations, were not about to spend the money necessary to build a television station until they knew that they could make a profit. Likewise, manufacturers would not start making television sets until there was some motivation for people to buy them, that is, regular programming to watch.

While great strides were being made in electronic television in America, in England, John Logie Baird's mechanical system was being used successfully by the BBC. In May 1931, the British network went mobile and filmed the first live street scenes for viewers. A few weeks later, Baird provided live coverage for the BBC of the English Derby, a famous horse race.

But the mechanical system's days were numbered. In 1936 the BBC considered Radio Marconi's all-electronic television system. The British corporation was quickly convinced that the newer system was far more efficient and better than Baird's was. Officials made the switch to electronic that year and Baird, one of the medium's great pioneers, was finished in television.

Back in America, 1936 was also a landmark year for television. NBC opened its first complete television studio at Rockefeller Center, where the network still has its headquarters today. The premiere broadcast was hosted by radio personality Betty Goodwin who introduced members of the dance troupe the Radio City Rockettes, comedian Ed Wynn, and a group of very pleased RCA executives. While the twenty-minute program was entertaining, it was not particularly viewable. Critics, such as *The New Yorker* magazine, complained that, when seen onscreen, people looked like they were underwater. At 343 scanned picture lines, a great improvement over the 60 lines of 1930, television still had a long way to go before providing a clear and sharp picture.

"The World of Tomorrow"

For the next few years, television remained mostly in the laboratory. The decade belonged to the movies, the public's favorite and main source of entertainment. Hollywood's dream factory turned out films that helped the American public forget their day-to-day troubles during the Depression that still gripped the nation.

Then in 1939, the year the Depression officially "ended," a world's fair was held in Queens, a borough of New York City. The theme of the

RCA PRESIDENT DAVID SARNOFF'S DEDICATION OF THE RCA PAVILION AT THE 1939 NEW YORK WORLD'S FAIR IS THE FIRST NEWS EVENT BROADCAST BY HIS FLEDGLING TELEVISION NETWORK, NBC.

THIS IS THE GRAINY IMAGE THAT FAIRGOERS AND NEW YORKERS SAW ON TELEVISION MONITORS SET UP AROUND THE CITY. WITHIN A SHORT TIME OF THIS HISTORIC BROADCAST, NEW YORKERS WITH THE NECESSARY FUNDS COULD BUY THEIR OWN TELEVISION SET.

fair was "The World of Tomorrow," and David Sarnoff and RCA were determined to make television a dominant force in this new world.

"Now we add radio sight to sound," Sarnoff, RCA's then president, announced at the debut of the company's pavilion at the fair on April 20, 1939. "[Television] is an art which shines like a torch of hope in a troubled world. It is a creative force which we must learn to utilize for the benefit of all mankind."

Ten days later, President Franklin D. Roosevelt became the first head of state to appear live on television at the fair. The television cameras were placed 50 feet (15.2 meters) from the president on the raised platform. The Secret Service, whose job it is to protect the president, would not allow them any closer. About one thousand people throughout the New York City area watched Roosevelt on television on two hundred receivers set up in various public venues.

After that, television became the talk of the fair. Fairgoers watched in awe as entertainers from Radio City Music Hall performed on screens for an hour two nights a week. Outdoor events at the fair itself were broadcast three afternoons a week.

Confident television was gaining the nation's attention, RCA extended its broadcasting to seven days a week and put their first television sets on sale. They ranged in cost from $200 to $1,000. The least expensive, still quite pricey for the average American, had a 4- by 5-inch (10- by 12.7-centimeter) screen. The top-end model boasted a 7- by 10-inch (17.8- by 25.4-centimeter) screen.

Those New Yorkers affluent enough to buy a set received a postcard with their purchase which they then had to send to RCA. In return, the company mailed each new television owner a card listing each week's program schedule. By the end of 1939, there were about 2,500 television set owners in the greater New York area.

The Birth of Commercial Television

April 30, 1941, was the day that David Sarnoff and his competitors at CBS had been waiting for. It was then that the FCC authorized unrestricted commercial television. Television stations were allowed to broadcast on eighteen channels. Channel one was reserved for the use of mobile police

If you were one of the few lucky owners of a television set in 1940, your television-viewing options would have been extremely restricted. Forget about the hundreds of channels currently available to cable subscribers. Your set would probably get just one channel, two at best. And for most of the day all you would be able to see was a test pattern with some background music. The broadcasting day did not begin until the afternoon and then consisted of a short movie or two. All the major Hollywood studios refused to sell their product to television stations, seeing it as a threat to their business. The movies shown came from minor or what today would be called B film studios and were generally of poor quality. When the movie ended, broadcasting ceased on W2XBS, only to return at 6:45 p.m. with a fifteen-minute newscast delivered by radio commentator Lowell Thomas. It was a simulcast of his radio program, and there were no visuals or on-the-scene reporting—just Thomas sitting at his desk reading the news.

If it was action you wanted, you only had a short wait for the centerpiece of 1940s television—sports. Basketball, hockey, and boxing were shown live from New York's Madison Square Garden. While the action in team sports was at times hard to follow due to the primitive camera set-ups, there were no commercials to interrupt the play. On Sunday nights television presented more cultural fare. NBC aired a live performance of a Broadway show or showcased top singers and comedians from Radio City Music Hall. All in all, a week's worth of television in 1940 was not enough to turn even the most avid viewer into a couch potato.

A BOY IS OVERJOYED TO BE WATCHING A BASEBALL GAME ON AN EARLY GENERAL ELECTRIC TELEVISION, CIRCA 1939. IN ACTUALITY, THE BROADCASTING OF MOST TEAM SPORTS WAS SEVERELY LIMITED BY STATIONARY CAMERAS. BUT TO THE FIRST GENERATION OF TELEVISION VIEWERS, IT STILL MUST HAVE SEEMED INCREDIBLE TO WATCH A SPORTING EVENT FROM THE COMFORT OF THEIR LIVING ROOMS.

and fire radios so they would not interfere with television transmissions. To this day, there are no stations broadcast on channel one. With this new development, NBC's W2XBS became WNBT, the nation's first commercial station. Its initial viewing audience was limited to about 4,700 households. By the end of 1941, however, sales of television sets reached the one million mark nationwide, and there was a total of twenty-one licensed stations across the country.

Unfortunately, this increased activity was short lived. On December 7, 1941, just five months after the FCC decision, Ray Forrest, WNBT's only full-time announcer, interrupted the broadcast of the movie *Millionaire Playboy* to tell viewers that the Japanese had attacked the American naval fleet stationed at Pearl Harbor in Hawaii. The next day President Franklin D. Roosevelt declared the United States at war with Japan and its allies, Germany and Italy. The nation's attention quickly turned away from television. Within weeks, nearly all regular television broadcasting was suspended. It would not return for another five years. Once again, a world war had brought the development of television to an abrupt halt.

THIS STYLISH WOMAN IS DELIGHTED WITH HER GENERAL ELECTRIC TELEVISION "PICTURE RECEIVER." SOME TELEVISION MANUFACTURERS COMPENSATED FOR THEIR TINY SCREEN BY MOUNTING A MAGNIFYING PLASTIC BUBBLE OVER IT.

From Novelty to National Pastime

After the attack on Pearl Harbor, the entire nation mobilized for war, and the two biggest television networks did their part too. David Sarnoff helped organize the communications lines that were used for the massive Allied invasion at the beaches of Normandy, France, on D-Day, June 6, 1944. For his contribution to this decisive victory, Sarnoff was appointed a brigadier general. The egotistical executive kept the title General Sarnoff for the rest of his life. Not to be outdone by Sarnoff, CBS's president William Paley produced informational war films for the Office of War Information using Hollywood actors and was conferred the rank of colonel for his efforts.

Although NBC and CBS suspended all regular commercial broadcasting during the war, television screens were not entirely blank from 1942 through 1945. The television station, started by inventor Allen Du Mont back in 1939 (later to become the Du Mont Network), continued to broadcast regularly throughout the war years. Its broadcast of updates on the war's progress provided an invaluable service to the American public.

Du Mont had created a state-of-the-art picture tube in his garage laboratory that lasted ten times longer than any other picture tube of the time. He gave RCA stiff competition in the early 1940s in the television set market. With backing from Paramount Pictures, a major Hollywood studio, Du Mont opened two television stations, one in New Jersey and another, bigger one in New York City.

Du Mont—
The Little Network
that Could

The Du Mont Network, formed in 1946, occupies a curious niche in the history of television. It was a broadcasting pioneer and innovator, the direct ancestor of the independent networks that sprang up in the late 1980s and 1990s.

Du Mont could not compete directly with the big-budget shows offered by NBC and CBS, so the network specialized in inexpensive but often creative programming. Along the way it scored a number of television firsts. In October 1946, it began airing the first daytime drama series, *Faraway Hill*. Because companies that made soap products sponsored many of these daytime dramas, they came to be called "soap operas." Du Mont debuted the first science-fiction series for children, the immensely popular *Captain Video*, in 1949 and the first network news show, *Walter Compton News*, which included reports from New York and Washington, D.C.

CAPTAIN VIDEO, STAR OF THE FIRST SCIENCE-FICTION SERIES FOR CHILDREN, TAKES AIM AT AN ALIEN ENEMY WITH A RAY GUN. *CAPTAIN VIDEO* THRILLED YOUNG VIEWERS ON THE DU MONT NETWORK FROM 1949 TO 1955 AND THEN RAN ONE MORE YEAR IN SYNDICATION. OTHER REGULARS ON THE SHOW INCLUDED THE CAPTAIN'S TEEN SIDEKICK, THE VIDEO RANGER, AND A ROBOT NAMED TOBOR (*ROBOT* SPELLED BACKWARD).

In 1950 Du Mont gave a little-known vaudeville comedian and film actor, Jackie Gleason, the opportunity to host its variety show *Cavalcade of Stars*. During his two-year stint on the program, Gleason created his classic sitcom *The Honeymooners*. In 1954 the network hired the brilliant and eccentric comic Ernie Kovacs to host a late-night comedy show and two quiz programs. Both Gleason and Kovacs would quickly move on, to CBS and NBC respectively, and become television stars.

Perhaps Du Mont's biggest find was its most unlikely one. Catholic bishop Fulton J. Sheen hosted a lecture-like series *Life Is Worth Living* on Tuesday nights. It was broadcast opposite comic Milton Berle's popular *Texaco Star Theater*. No one expected Sheen's program to last a season, but the show became a surprise hit and competed head to head with Berle for years.

But for all of its innovations, Du Mont was unable to overcome its shortcomings—a lack of radio affiliates that could support its television broadcasting. Then in 1953, Du Mont was dealt another blow when upstart network, the American Broadcasting Company (ABC), gained the support of Paramount. The FCC ruled that only seven U.S. cities could have as many as four television stations, and Du Mont, the fourth network, was squeezed out by ABC in most major urban markets. In September 1955 the network stopped broadcasting. Three years later it was reorganized as the Metropolitan Broadcasting Corporation and for three decades remained the largest independent group of stations in American television. Publishing magnate Rupert Murdoch bought the company in 1985 and it became Fox, the new fourth network, whose own innovations in programming matched those of its long-forgotten predecessor.

The Return of Television

When World War II ended on September 2, 1945, with Japan's surrender, television was ready to return to the airwaves. All three networks resumed regular broadcasting by 1946.

The country was experiencing a post-war economic boom. Americans wanted to enjoy new products that would make life easier and more enjoyable. Near the top of the list was television. RCA unveiled its new all-electronic television set, the 630. Appropriately named, it featured 630 scanned lines of picture, making it far superior in quality to pre-war receivers. The price of sets was still relatively expensive, however, and most Americans waited for them to become more affordable. But this did not stop them from watching television whenever and wherever they could.

Bars and clubs did a booming business as patrons crowded in to watch boxing and wrestling and other sporting events on television. Those who did not frequent bars could stand outside appliance stores and watch a program on the demonstration sets placed in the windows. Or those who were lucky enough to have a neighbor with a television might be invited over to watch, as the author's parents were back in 1948. Every Tuesday night they went to their neighbors' apartment in Queens, New York, to watch *Texaco Star Theater,* hosted by Milton Berle (more on him later). "It was such a treat. We looked forward to that one evening all week," recalls Helen Otfinoski. "To think you could sit in someone's livingroom and watch television. We were in awe."

THIS YOUNGSTER LOOKS ON IN AWE AT A DEMONSTRATION TELEVISION SET IN A STORE WINDOW. MANY AMERICANS IN THE LATE 1940S GOT THEIR FIRST GLIMPSE OF TELEVISION IN A SIMILAR FASHION. THE WINDOW DISPLAYS HELPED SELL THOUSANDS OF SETS.

Wrestling on Television

If you could use only one word to explain the sudden sales of television sets in the United States immediately after World War II, that word would be *wrestling*. Wrestling was not only the first and most popular sport shown on television, it was the medium's most popular entertainment. In some cities wrestling aired every night of the week. Why? Part of the reason was pure logistics. Other sports such as basketball and football featured players moving over a large area, difficult for the stationary cameras of the time to capture. In wrestling, a single camera could catch all the action of two opponents fighting in a small ring. Boxing had the same advantage, but it appealed mostly to men, while wrestling drew both female and male viewers. Viewers liked the antics of the colorful participants and while boxing could be bloody, wrestlers were rarely hurt. That was because most of the matches were rigged.

Television wrestling was more show business than sport, thanks in large part to George Wagner (also known as Gorgeous George), a wrestler who became famous for his long blonde hair, colorful silk robes, and outrageous behavior. George set the pattern, and every wrestler who wanted to become a television star looked for a gimmick of his own. Among the other better known wrestlers featured were Baron Leone, Antonio "Argentina" Rocca, and Farmer Jones, who entered the ring carrying a pig.

If Gorgeous George was the king of the wrestlers, than Dennis James was the king of wrestling announcers. To jazz up the proceedings, James would add sound effects, tearing a window shade when a wrestler tugged on his trunks or twisting a chicken bone to make a crackling sound when one wrestler wrenched the leg of his opponent.

James even stepped into the ring himself on one memorable occasion to take on wrestler Bibber McCoy as part of a stunt. When McCoy put a chokehold on him, James passed out, live on the air. "They slapped me around," James later recalled, "and when I came to I was all disheveled, but I completed the show."

What were all these people watching on the set? Besides sports and variety shows, most programming was simple, shot on one set, to accommodate the stationary cameras and modest programming budgets. The television schedule abounded in quiz and game shows, children's puppet shows, and news programs. All these programs were produced by local stations, affiliates of the networks. There was as yet no such thing as a "national broadcast." The technology to send a television signal across the nation did not yet exist. The only way to broadcast a program in another region of the country was to lit-

WRESTLER GEORGE WAGNER, BETTER KNOWN TO TELEVISION VIEWERS AS GORGEOUS GEORGE, WAS ONE OF THE MEDIUM'S FIRST SUPERSTARS. HE WAS ALWAYS ACCOMPANIED INTO THE RING BY A MALE VALET WHO SPRAYED HIS CORNER AND HIS OPPONENT WITH DISINFECTANT AND PERFUME.

erally film it off a television screen as it was broadcast. This film, called a kine-scope, could then be air mailed to another station and broadcast. The quality of kinescopes was notoriously bad, though, and the image was murky at best.

Howdy, Hoppy, Uncle Miltie, and a Really Big Show

Between late 1947 and early 1949, television produced four of its first major stars. This unlikely quartet was composed of a freckled-faced marionette, an aging B-western cowboy star, a corny vaudeville comic, and a tongue-tied Broadway columnist.

The Howdy Doody Show, the first network children's program, pre-miered on NBC in 1947. Hosted by "Buffalo" Bob Smith, one of the few humans who inhabited the show's setting of Doodyville, it also featured an array of puppets, including Howdy, the star; Mr. Bluster, the dyspep-tic mayor of Doodyville; and Flubadub, a strange creature made up of the parts of eight different animals. There was also Clarabelle, a mute clown who periodically squirted people with seltzer water. The first Clarabelle was Bob Keeshan, who would go on to become famous as the title character in another successful children's program *Captain Kan-garoo.* But perhaps what really made *Howdy Doody* such a hit was its live audience of children, who sat in an area called the Peanut Gallery. Being on the show became so popular that parents put their kids on a waiting list sometimes before they were even born. Howdy Doody ran for thirteen years. On the final show in 1960, Clarabelle finally spoke. With a tear in his eye he said, "Good-bye, kids."

If Howdy was fun, Hopalong Cassidy meant action and adventure. William Boyd, a former silent screen star, had played western hero Hopalong Cassidy, better know as Hoppy, in a long string of B-pictures from the mid-1930s through 1947. While most Hollywood studios re-fused to sell their film libraries to television, Boyd had the foresight to see the potential television offered and sold the rights to most of his

WHAT TIME IS IT, KIDS? EVERY BABY BOOOMER THAT GREW UP IN THE 1950S KNEW THE ANSWER TO THAT QUESTION: "HOWDY DOODY TIME!" STAR OF THE FIRST HIT NETWORK CHILDREN'S PROGRAM, HOWDY'S VOICE WAS PROVIDED BY HUMAN HOST "BUFFALO" BOB SMITH, WHO PRERECORDED IT SO HE COULD SING DUETS WITH THE PUPPET.

features to NBC for $350,000 per film. The Hoppy westerns became a staple of early television and were so popular that Boyd filmed forty new episodes. He also licensed Hoppy's image to sell a wealth of merchandise from wristwatches to cowboy hats to pajamas. The millions he made off these products showed just how powerful a selling tool television could be.

Milton Berle, a veteran comic of stage, film, and radio, was just one of several hosts who were considered for *Texaco Star Theater,* an NBC variety show that debuted in the summer of 1948. Berle, who had appeared on experimental television as early as 1929, got the job as permanent host with his corny jokes, his outrageous costumes (he loved to dress in drag), and his rapport with the live audience. For three seasons, Berle and the *Texaco Star Theater* dominated Tuesday nights, at one point getting nearly 95 percent share of the television audience. On Tuesday nights, bars, clubs, and other public venues were nearly empty. Practically everyone was home huddled around the set watching Uncle Miltie, as he called himself. Berle's popularity sold literally millions of television sets, earning him another nickname, Mr. Television. *Texaco Star Theater* remains the most popular variety show in television history.

That same season, another variety show debuted on CBS that would far outlast *Texaco Star Theater. Toast of the Town* (renamed *The Ed Sullivan Show* in 1955) was hosted by Ed Sullivan. He was an odd choice for the job since he was not a performer (he wrote a column for a New York newspaper), had no stage presence, and regularly fumbled his introductions with his mispronunciations and unique intonation ("a really big show" came out "a really big shoe"). But audiences found Sullivan's unpolished on-air persona endearing and, because he was not a traditional performer, they did not grow tired of his "act." Sullivan was also a shrewd judge of talent and packed his hourly show with acts to appeal to every taste and temperament. He gave singer Elvis Presley his first important national exposure in 1956 and introduced the British rock band the Beatles to American audiences in 1964. A typical Sullivan show might have on the bill a ventriloquist, a couple of stand-up comics, a Metropolitan Opera star singing an aria, and a family juggling act. For twenty-three years, *The Ed Sullivan Show* was a Sunday night institution, when Americans flocked to their televisions to watch the variety of offerings that helped make the show a hit.

And Now for the News . . .

News programs, many of them consisting of an announcer reading news bulletins or filmed newsreels, became popular in the early post-war years.

ED SULLIVAN IS PRESENTING ANOTHER "REALLY BIG SHOW" FOR HIS TELEVISION AUDIENCE. WHILE A MASTER SHOW-MAN, SULLIVAN WAS SO RIGID IN FRONT OF CAMERAS THAT HE WAS NICKNAMED "OLD STONE FACE." A GENERATION OF COMEDIANS MADE GOOD LIVINGS IMPERSONATING HIS AWKWARD MANNERISMS AND VERBAL GOOFS.

John Cameron Swayze—an actor, game show host, and commercial pitchman—became the first well-known news anchor on NBC's *The Camel Newsreel Theater* in 1948 (later to be renamed *The Camel News Caravan*). "That's the story, folks," he would say at the end of each broadcast. "Glad we could be together!" *The CBS-TV News* boasted a real newsman as anchor, Douglas Edwards, but unlike NBC it had no commercial sponsor to pay the show's costs. No potential sponsors felt that people would turn to television for their news. This national evening news program ran for fifteen minutes until CBS expanded its coverage to thirty minutes in 1963.

Television was also slowly being seen as a medium that could capture news events as they were unfolding. On October 5, 1947, Harry Truman became the first U.S. president to make a live televised address from the White House. In November 1948, television covered the presidential election results in the race between Truman and Republican challenger Thomas E. Dewey. NBC actually delayed its election coverage until *Texaco Star Theater* was over. Entertainment won out easily over politics and news.

Truman's second inauguration in March 1949 was the first ever to be televised. "More Americans have seen President Truman by television in one evening than saw Lincoln during his entire term in the White House," boasted David Sarnoff.

The Emmy Awards

In 1946 reporter Syd Cassyd founded the Academy of Television Arts and Sciences to show that television could be as respectable a medium as film or radio. In January 1949, the academy hosted its first annual awards for the 1948–1949 television season. The awards statue, designed by a television engineer who modeled it after his wife, was first called "Ike," short for iconoscope. The name was then feminized to "Immy" to avoid confusion with the name of the World War II general Dwight "Ike" Eisenhower. Eventually the name transformed into the one used today—Emmy.

The awards dinner was held at the Hollywood Athletic Club and tickets were $5. Few Hollywood celebrities bothered to show up, and only six Emmys were awarded. The first went to twenty-year-old ventriloquist Shirley Dinsdale, whose children's show *Judy Splinters* was a hit in Los Angeles. The best television program award went to *Pantomime Quiz,* and the technical award was given to Chuck Mesak for inventing the phasefader, a machine that changed the colors on title cards from white to black and from black to white. All the nominated programs originated in Los Angeles, which started a feud with the New York television stations that would continue for years.

As the 1940s came to a close, it was clear that television was not a passing fad, but was here to stay. The number of television sets in American households had grown from less than 10,000 in 1945 to about six million in 1950. Television was about to enter what many would call its "golden age."

THE MOST COVETED AWARD IN TELEVISION, THE FIRST EMMYS WERE AWARDED IN 1949 FOR THE PAST YEAR'S PROGRAMMING. FRUSTRATED THAT WEST COAST TELEVISION STATIONS DOMINATED THE AWARDS, THE EAST COAST STATIONS CREATED THEIR OWN AWARDS AND CALLED THEM THE "MICHAELS," FOR MICROPHONE. THE MICHAEL AWARDS WERE GIVEN OUT ONLY ONE YEAR BEFORE THE IDEA WAS DROPPED.

THREE COUPLES IN PHILADELPHIA WATCH PRESIDENT HARRY TRUMAN ADDRESS THE UNITED NATIONS IN OCTOBER 1946. TRUMAN WOULD ENJOY MANY TELEVISION FIRSTS AS PRESIDENT, INCLUDING GIVING THE FIRST TELEVISED TOUR OF THE WHITE HOUSE IN 1952, WHICH INCLUDED PLAYING A MOZART PIECE ON THE PIANO FOR THE TELEVISION CAMERAS IN THE EAST ROOM.

FOUR

The Golden Age

On September 4, 1951, television entered a new era. For the first time, an estimated 20 million television viewers from coast to coast watched a broadcast event—President Truman addressing the opening of the Japanese Peace Treaty Conference in San Francisco—simultaneously. This feat was achieved by the construction of 107 steel-and-concrete towers set 28 miles (45 kilometers) apart between San Francisco and New York City, the nerve center of television broadcasting. The towers passed the television signals by way of microwave relays.

"The President could be seen as clearly on this end of the 3,000-mile [4,828-kilometer] hookup as if he had been speaking from the studios of a New York station," wrote one reporter for an East Coast newspaper, "and probably better than from rear seats in the War Memorial Opera House where he delivered his address."

That same year, *See It Now,* a CBS news program, debuted with a dramatic display of intercontinental television. One side of a split screen showed a live picture of New York's Brooklyn Bridge and the other the Golden Gate Bridge in San Francisco. Senior CBS newsman Edward R. Murrow intoned over the images, "We are impressed by a medium through which a man sitting in his living room has been able for the first time to look at two oceans at once."

No longer would television be a local affair, with each station generating most of its own programming. No longer would viewers around the country have to strain their eyes to watch fuzzy kinescopes filmed off a receiver of programs originating from New York or Los Angeles. Now the same clear signal could be sent simultaneously across the nation. The networks took over the prime-time viewing hours of 7:30 to 11 p.m., and local programs were relegated to the daytime and late evening hours.

We Loved Lucy

The advent of coast-to-coast television came as CBS launched the most popular program since Milton Berle's *Texaco Star Theater*. Film actress Lucille Ball had been playing a ditzy housewife on the radio sitcom *My Favorite Wife,* when the network invited her to reprise the role in a television series. Ball agreed, but only on the condition that her real-life husband, Cuban bandleader Desi Arnaz, play her husband. CBS turned her down, saying the audiences would never accept Arnaz as her husband and that his accent would make him unintelligible. To prove CBS wrong, the couple produced their own pilot for the series and took it on the road, playing it live before audiences across the country. The response was favorable, and the pilot convinced the network to let Desi play bandleader Ricky Ricardo.

But there were other challenges to face. Lucy and Desi wanted to do the show, now called *I Love Lucy*, in Los Angeles and not New York, where most series were produced live. Since the method for the coast-to-coast transmission of regular programs was still being perfected, CBS balked. Executives did not want to have to send fuzzy kinescopes to the rest of the country. Arnaz suggested filming the sitcom live, something that had not been attempted before on television. CBS agreed, and each show was filmed before a live audience like a play, in three acts, with multiple cameras catching the action. Afterward, each episode was edited down and sent as high-quality film to other stations for broadcast. This same format is still used today in filming most television sitcoms, although videotape has since replaced film.

I Love Lucy set a new standard for television entertainment. The scripts were first-rate, production values excellent, and Lucy proved a classic clown and comedian. In its second season, *I Love Lucy* became the number one show on television, a position it retained for three seasons. When the first issue of *TV Guide,* a new magazine devoted to the medium, appeared in 1952, Lucy and Desi were pictured on the cover.

Desi convinced the network to make Lucy's real-life pregnancy a part of the show's story line in the second season, breaking ground in television yet again. By remarkable coincidence, Ball's baby was born the same day "little Ricky" was born on television. The next morning the "double birth" made bigger headlines in the nation's newspapers than the inauguration of President Dwight D. Eisenhower.

LUCILLE BALL AND DESI ARNAZ, TELEVISION'S FIRST COUPLE, PRODUCED THE MOST POPULAR SERIES IN TELEVISION HISTORY, *I LOVE LUCY.* DESPITE THEIR AMOUROUS POSE HERE, THE COUPLE DIVORCED IN 1960, AND LUCY CONTINUED ON HER OWN, DELIGHTING TV VIEWERS FOR TWELVE MORE SEASONS ON *THE LUCY SHOW* AND *HERE'S LUCY.*

The Arnazes formed their own studio, Desilu, and soon became the top producer of hit television series. These included the sitcoms *Our Miss Brooks* and *The Danny Thomas Show,* as well as the pioneering period gangster drama *The Untouchables,* which set a new standard for violence on television.

Live from New York

While Desilu was revolutionizing the way television was filmed, most of television programming was still being broadcast live. In 1952, 82 percent of all network programs were live. That included everything from variety shows to dramas to game shows. Live television was demanding, difficult, and often intimidating for the actors. Anything could go wrong and often did. A prop could fail, an actor could forget his lines, or a camera could malfunction. But no matter what happened, the program had to go on.

"It was tension, tension, tension, all the way," recalled producer and writer Max Wilk. "When you put the show on, you sat there and you prayed that it would work, because you had no control on a live show."

Live drama, a staple of 1950s television, was particularly difficult to produce. Getting actors from one scene to the next, in another part of the crowded studio, was often a logistical nightmare. The stage manager would crawl across the studio floor to tap an actor on the ankle to let him or her know that they were off camera and that it was time to run to another set for the next scene.

Actor panic was a common occurrence. "The worst time was thirty seconds before you go on," remembered actor Rod Steiger. "At that time, if somebody showed you an open door you'd run home to your mother. Part of me is saying 'I can't remember, I won't remember, I won't remember.' The other part is 'Whatamidoinghere? Whatamidoinghere? Whatamidoinghere? Oh God, my friends are gonna see me.'"

Yet despite all the problems, actors turned in astonishing performances, many of which are still remembered today, half a century later. At its best, "live television" brought a raw, unforgettable immediacy and excitement to television that videotape and film have not been able to recapture.

The Army-McCarthy Hearings

Not all the drama on 1950s television was fictional. In 1951 Senator Estes Kefauver allowed television cameras for the first time into Senate

Golden Age Drama

committee hearings investigating organized crime. One witness who appeared before the committee was alleged New York crime czar Frank Costello. Costello refused to allow the cameras to show his face, claiming it violated his rights. So instead, the cameras focused on Costello's hands, which twitched nervously as he denied that he was involved in organized crime. His hands condemned him and the Kefauver hearings became television's first hit "reality show."

A far greater drama was acted out in Washington, D.C., before television cameras three years later. Senator Joseph McCarthy of Wisconsin had risen to national prominence for his relentless attacks on Communists in American society. A true demagogue, who had little real evidence to support his accusations, McCarthy went after Communist sympathizers he claimed were in the State Department and other governmental agencies.

Few people, including President Eisenhower, were willing to stand up and oppose McCarthy's witchhunt. His power seemed to make him untouchable. One of the few who dared take him on was Edward

It was live drama that put the gold in the golden age of television. The first live weekly drama anthology was the *Ford Television Theater*. It premiered on CBS in the fall of 1948. By the 1955–56 season, there were sixteen live drama series in prime time. At first, these shows consisted mostly of adaptations of Broadway plays. When television producers tried to get rights to classic Hollywood movies to adapt, however, the studios turned them down. Then top producers like Fred Coe turned to fresh, young writers with little or no experience to create original television dramas. An extraordinary generation of gifted writers was discovered, including Paddy Chayefesky, Gore Vidal, Reginald Rose, and Rod Serling.

The actors were also young and ambitious, many of them straight from the New York stage. Many would go on to become film stars—Paul Newman, James Dean, Jack Lemmon, Joanne Woodward, Grace Kelly, and Rod Steiger among them. Ironically, some of the best of the television dramas, including *Twelve Angry Men*, *Marty*, and *Requiem for a Heavyweight*, would go on to become successful Hollywood films. *Marty*, the story of a lonely butcher who finds love at a dance, won four Academy Awards, including one for best picture.

But just as the golden age was reaching its peak, it fell into decline. By the mid-1950s filmed series from California, many of them westerns and crime shows, were beginning to replace live drama. Filmed shows were easy to produce, had few technical problems, and could be shown again and again in reruns, bringing in far more money than a single live broadcast. By 1961 only 18 percent of all network programs were live. Yet the legacy of the golden age continued into the 1960s as the era's writers produced thoughtful filmed series such as Reginald Rose's courtroom drama *The Defenders* and Rod Serling's fantasy series *The Twilight Zone*.

MILLIONS OF AMERICANS WATCHED SPELLBOUND AS SENATOR JOSEPH MCCARTHY CARRIED HIS COMMUNIST WITCH-HUNT TO THE PENTAGON IN THE TELEVISED MCCARTHY-ARMY HEARINGS OF 1954. THE HEARINGS PROVED TO BE AS DRAMATICALLY ENGROSSING AS ANY FICTIONAL PROGRAM.

R. Murrow. A highly respected figure in broadcasting, Murrow went after McCarthy on a March 1954 edition of *See It Now*. "This is no time for men who oppose Senator McCarthy's methods to keep silent," Murrow declared. "We can deny our heritage and our history, but we cannot escape responsibility for the result." It was one of television's shining hours.

History, and television, finally caught up with McCarthy a month later. Confident in his unchecked power, McCarthy went after the U.S. Army, claiming that there were Communists within its ranks. The Senate committee of which McCarthy was a member conducted hearings on the charges leveled against the Army. Joseph Welch, a Boston lawyer, was retained to defend the Army. ABC, the smallest network, which had little daytime programming to pre-empt, agreed to broadcast the entire hearings. For the next three months, the Army-McCarthy hearings became riveting viewing for millions of Americans, even those with little interest in politics.

Welch showed McCarthy's charges to be largely empty. As the senator grew more desperate, he attacked a young lawyer in Welch's law office. Welch's response was worthy of a golden age television drama:

> Until this moment Senator, I think I never really gauged your cruelty or your recklessness. . . . If it were in my power to forgive you from your reckless cruelty, I would do so. I like to think that I am a gentle man, but your forgiveness will have to come from someone other than me. [McCarthy tried to clarify his accusations but Welch would have none of it.] Have you no sense of decency, sir, at long last? Have you left no sense of decency?

Welch and the television cameras had exposed McCarthy as the self-serving demagogue that he was. That December he was officially censured by the Senate and three years later died, a hopeless alcoholic.

Morning, Noon, and Late Night

In the early years of television, daytime programming was limited. Many stations did not begin the broadcast day until late afternoon. Often there was no programming in the early morning or after 11 p.m. Many in the television industry felt people would not watch television at these early or late hours. Sylvester "Pat" Weaver, an executive at NBC, felt otherwise.

Weaver, a former radio executive known for creative innovations, wanted to invent programming unique to television that would show it to be more than, as he liked to put it, "radio with pictures." In 1952 he created *Today,* an early morning show of news, weather, light entertainment, and features that appealed to women on such subjects as cooking and home decorating. Weaver envisioned the three-hour program (later reduced to two) as drawing a drop-in audience that would watch briefly while eating breakfast and getting ready for school or work. Initial ratings were poor, but in *Today*'s second season Weaver brought in a

TODAY HOST DAVE GARROWAY POSES WITH TRAINED CHIMP FRED J. MUGGS. THE FIRST EARLY MORNING NETWORK PROGRAM, TODAY WAS A RATINGS FAILURE UNTIL THE CHIMP JOINED THE CAST. HOWEVER, GARROWAY'S RELAXED AND INTIMATE STYLE HAD MORE LASTING IMPORTANCE THAN MUGGS'S ANTICS.

trained chimpanzee named J. Fred Muggs in an attempt to lure additional viewers. Muggs helped make the show a hit, and he was a regular performer for four years. Still on the air, *Today* remains one of the longest-running programs in television history and one of the most profitable.

Weaver's attempt at a midday program, *Home*, was less successful. This so-called "women's magazine of the air" debuted in 1954 and lasted only three years. The idea of a television magazine, however, was used a decade later by CBS, when it created *60 Minutes*, the prototype for all subsequent news magazine programs.

Weaver's attempt at airing a successful late-night variety-type show seemed just as tenuous. His *Broadway Open House* debuted in 1950 and lasted little more than a year. He tried again in 1953 with *Tonight!*, which had a more sophisticated format and featured host Steve Allen, a cast of regulars, and guest stars. Allen's gift for adlib and his wacky humor kept many New York viewers up until 1 a.m. most weekday nights. The program went national a year and a half later, and Allen left the show for prime time in 1957. The second host of the show, now named *The Tonight Show*, was a little-known radio and television comic and personality named Jack Paar. He brought an intimacy and seriousness to the program, making it more of a talk show. Intense and emotional, viewers either hated him or loved him. When NBC censored a harmless joke about bathrooms in February 1960, Paar walked off the set the following evening. He returned a month later with the classic line "as I was saying before I was interrupted . . ."

Paar left *The Tonight Show* permanently in 1962 and was replaced by midwestern comic and television game show host Johnny Carson. Carson was laid back and easygoing where Paar had been passionate and intense. Accused by some of being bland, Carson made his guests and audience comfortable, and they remained his loyal followers for an incredible thirty years. By the time he hosted his last *Tonight Show* on May 22, 1992, Carson was a television legend, known for his topical opening monologue and his generosity to new talent. Comic Jay Leno has hosted the show since Carson's retirement, and it remains the number-one television late night program.

Hollywood Enters the Picture

The Hollywood studios, with the exception of Columbia, remained television's enemy throughout the early 1950s. When a television set appeared in a Hollywood movie, it was usually an object of satire. Jack Warner, head of Warner Brothers Studios, hated television so passionately that he would not let his wife watch it.

Then in October 1954, Walt Disney, the head of Disney Studios, produced an hour-long show *Disneyland* for ABC. It would later be known by other names and subsequently be aired on the other two networks. The show was perfectly timed to promote Disney's new California

THE *MICKEY MOUSE CLUB* WAS THE FIRST POPULAR CHILDREN'S PROGRAM TO FEATURE CHILD PERFORMERS, THE MOUSKETEERS, AS ITS STARS. ANNETTE, THE MOST POPULAR MOUSKETEER, WENT ON TO BECOME A POPULAR RECORDING ARTIST AND THE STAR OF A STRING OF TEEN BEACH MOVIES IN THE 1960S. THE FELLOW WITH THE GUITAR AND THE BIG SMILE IS ADULT HOST JIMMY DODD.

Rise of the Western

Westerns had been a television staple since Hopalong Cassidy first rode across the small screen in 1949. But early television westerns such as *The Lone Ranger* and *The Cisco Kid* were primarily aimed at children.

In 1955 *Gunsmoke* debuted along with *Cheyenne* as the first of the "adult" westerns. They featured more realistic plots and deeper characterizations. Soon westerns were the dominant dramatic genre on television. By the 1957–1958 season, nine westerns were among the top twenty-five shows. By March 1959, eight of the top ten shows were "horse operas," as the genre was often called.

Western heroes were so plentiful that it took an enticing gimmick to stand out from the rest of the pack. In some westerns the hero had a unique weapon to fight the bad guys with. Sometimes the weapon was referred to in the series' title. *The Rifleman*, *Shotgun Slade*, *Yancy Derringer*, and *Colt 45* captivated scores of viewers. For those viewers who liked their westerns less violent, there was even a show called *Man without a Gun* about a crusading newspaper editor in the Old West.

While few of these shows measured up to the live drama series they had replaced, a surprising number were well made, captured the rugged spirit of the Old West, and were filled with action and suspense. Some leading western actors went on to become major film stars, including Clint Eastwood (*Rawhide*), Steve McQueen (*Wanted: Dead or Alive*), and James Garner (*Maverick*).

Gunsmoke, one of the first adult westerns, outlived all of the competition. CBS finally cancelled it after twenty seasons, not because of poor ratings, but because its audience largely consisted of older Americans, a group that did not strongly appeal to most sponsors. Today, with the exception of a few television movies and mini-series, the western, along with the variety show and the drama anthology, has virtually disappeared from network programming.

ONE OF THE FIRST AND MOST POPULAR CHILDREN'S TELEVISION WESTERNS, *THE LONE RANGER* WAS FAMOUS FOR ITS MASKED HERO PLAYED BY CLAYTON MOORE, WHO ONLY FIRED SILVER BULLETS AT THE BAD GUYS, AND ITS THEME MUSIC, THE STIRRING "WILLIAM TELL OVERTURE." THE RANGER'S FAITHFUL INDIAN SIDEKICK TONTO WAS PLAYED BY REAL NATIVE AMERICAN JAY SILVERHEELS.

theme park of the same name. It also helped promote the company's upcoming movies. *Disneyland* became the first ABC series to break into the top twenty of the highest-rated programs. The show was so successful that a few years later Disney produced *The Mickey Mouse Club*, an afternoon children's program.

Jack Warner took note and in 1955 started producing a variety of one-hour action-adventure series for ABC. The western *Cheyenne* proved the most successful of these and was the first of a string of popular adult westerns and detective dramas produced on the Warner lot. By 1958 Warner Brothers was producing ten hours of prime-time programming each week for ABC.

The Warner Brothers series were all filmed on high-quality videotape, a new technological development. While some shows were well written, overall the quality was below that of the live drama anthologies that had preceded them. Part of this compromised quality was due to the show's sponsors, who now had a bigger say in the programs they were paying for. They wanted nothing controversial that might offend any segment of the viewing audience. This led to bland scripts and often handsome but generic protagonists.

When Newton Minow, the head of the Federal Communications Commission (FCC), sat down to watch a day's worth of television in 1961 he declared what he saw was "a vast wasteland" consisting of "a procession of game shows, violence, audience participation shows, formula comedies about totally unbelievable families, blood and thunder, mayhem, violence . . . and cartoons." For some discriminating viewers, it appeared that the golden age was over. But television's influence and power would continue to grow. It had become a national habit that proved difficult for viewers to break. As legendary filmmaker and radio pioneer Orson Welles said, "I hate television. I hate it as much as peanuts. But I cannot stop eating peanuts."

THE NIXON-KENNEDY PRESIDENTIAL DEBATES IN 1960 WERE A DEFINING MOMENT FOR THE COMING TOGETHER OF TELEVISION AND POLITICS. IN THIS, THE THIRD DEBATE, THE CANDIDATES FACED OFF FROM OPPOSITE COASTS—NIXON IN LOS ANGELES AND KENNEDY IN NEW YORK.

The Global Village

Nineteen sixty was a watershed year in American politics and in American television as well. For the first time, the two major candidates for president would face off in four, live televised debates. Some 75 million Americans tuned in to watch the first debate on September 26, 1960, between Republican Richard Nixon and Democrat John F. Kennedy. Nixon, who had served eight years as vice president under President Dwight D. Eisenhower, was perceived as the more experienced and knowledgeable candidate. Many Americans knew little or nothing about Kennedy, a senator from Massachusetts. That all changed after the first debate.

Kennedy looked relaxed, youthful, and exuded a certain charisma before the television cameras. Nixon, in contrast, looked tired, appeared unshaven, and wore a gray suit that made him recede into the background of the set.

Interestingly, those who watched the first debate on television chose Kennedy as the clear winner, while radio listeners believed Nixon had won. The power of television made Kennedy a national figure overnight, and although Nixon became more savvy before the cameras in the subsequent debates, it was not enough to sway the electorate. In November, during the most televised presidential election night to that time,

Kennedy narrowly defeated Nixon and won the presidency. From that moment on, television would be the most important platform for any politician seeking national office.

The First Television President

"We wouldn't have had a prayer without that gadget," Kennedy later said, acknowledging television's role in his victory. Not surprisingly, he quickly proved to be a master of the medium. Handsome and charming, with a sense of humor that won over many members of the media, Kennedy became the first president to permit live television coverage of all of his news conferences. First Lady Jackie Kennedy was youthful, stylish, and as popular as her husband was. Her tour of the White House, televised as a special on CBS, was one of the most talked-about shows of the 1961–1962 season.

In October 1962, the Soviets were discovered to be sending missiles to Communist ally Cuba to be installed only 70 miles (113 kilometers) from American shores. Kennedy went live on television on October 22 to tell the nation that he had ordered the Soviet Union to turn back the ships bringing the missiles. The Soviets heeded the warning, and the Cuban Missile Crisis had a peaceful resolution. Just a year later Kennedy met a tragic death at the hand of a lone assassin. "The television president" became the first major figure to be mourned on national television.

Television as Teacher

The potential for television to be an educational tool as well as a dispenser of news was realized early on. In 1952 the FCC set aside a group of channels for educational programming, and the Ford Foundation provided funds to set up a production center called National Educational Television (NET). But many of these stations failed, and educational television, or public television, as it came to be called, did not really become a force in the medium until New York City's independent

The Kennedy Assassination

When President Kennedy was shot shortly after noon in Dallas, Texas, on November 22, 1963, television was slow to relay the news. Although there were reporters and television cameras following Kennedy's motorcade when the shooting occurred, there were no immediate pictures of the actual shooting. Television news was still in its adolescence. CBS had become the first network to expand its evening newscast from fifteen to thirty minutes only a month earlier. The network's radio had actually reported Kennedy's death eighteen minutes before CBS anchorman Walter Cronkite made the televised announcement. (The network was waiting for a confirmation from a press source.)

It was only in the long, saddening aftermath of Kennedy's death that television began to exert its power. In an unprecedented move, all three networks suspended regular programming and commercials for the next four days. They ran tapes of Kennedy speeches and doggedly reported the hunt and capture of his killer, Lee Harvey Oswald.

On Sunday, as Oswald was being transferred from the city jail to the county jail, Jack Ruby, a Dallas nightclub owner, stepped out from behind a reporter and shot Oswald in the stomach as a horrified nation watched on live television. Oswald died shortly after. Over that unforgettable weekend, the average home watched 31.6 hours of coverage, according to an A. C. Neilson survey. On Monday, all three networks pooled their resources to broadcast the Kennedy funeral, offering up indelible images of the courageous widow and her two young children. Some 93 percent of all American homes watched the funeral on television. Satellite carried the event to 23 countries and more than 600 million viewers.

The suspension of commercials had cost the networks millions in revenue, but what they gained in prestige was incalculable. Even Newton Minow, the man who two years earlier had called television "a vast wasteland," was deeply impressed. "We always hear that television is a young medium," he said. "If so, it grew up in a couple of days."

Television, rather than the press or radio, had been the central medium for a nation in mourning. It had informed, shocked, and most important of all, comforted Americans grieving over their great loss. From that point on, when people wanted to know what was happening in the nation and the world, they would turn first to their television sets.

LEE HARVEY OSWALD, ALLEGED ASSASSIN OF PRESIDENT JOHN KENNEDY, IS WAYLAID BY THE MEDIA AS HE IS BEING ESCORTED FROM THE CITY TO THE COUNTY JAIL IN DALLAS, TEXAS. SHORTLY AFTER THIS PHOTOGRAPH WAS TAKEN, OSWALD WAS FATALLY SHOT BY NIGHTCLUB OWNER JACK RUBY. NBC-TV CAPTURED THE SHOCKING EVENT LIVE.

AN ATTENTIVE CLASSROOM OF FIRST GRADERS IN NEW YORK CITY WATCHES *THE SCIENCE CORNER,* AN EARLY EDUCATIONAL PROGRAM BROADCAST ON A LOCAL STATION IN 1957. EDUCATIONAL TELEVISION WOULD REMAIN SOMETHING OF A CURIOSITY UNTIL THE PUBLIC BROADCASTING ACT WAS PASSED A DECADE LATER.

Channel 13 became its flagship station in 1962. The Public Broadcasting Act of 1967 introduced a whole range of programming for public television that included not only classroom lectures but also documentaries, plays, concerts, and a wealth of cultural programs from Great Britain. Through the next decade, PBS (Public Broadcasting Service) would draw in millions of new viewers with its innovative, intelligent programming. *Sesame Street,* which debuted in November 1969, used puppets, comedy skits, songs, and guest stars to teach preschoolers the rudiments of reading, writing, and arithmetic. It remains one of the most praised and watched children's programs almost four decades later.

Commercial television had its own outstanding informational programs. CBS led the way with its award-winning *CBS Reports,* which has appeared sporadically since 1959. This hard-hitting, thoroughly researched documentary series was often narrated by Edward R. Murrow in its early years. Its greatest hour may have been *Harvest of Shame* (1960), about the unjust treatment of migrant workers in Florida. A successful foray into the news documentary, the classic program has been rebroadcast and updated over the years. Another mainstream hit for CBS was *The National Drivers' Test,* the first of many viewer-participation shows that tested viewer's knowledge on important topics and issues.

Innovative Dramas

Although television's Golden Age of Drama was over, there were new filmed dramatic series that took on serious issues as effectively as the best documentaries. *The Defenders* (1961–1965), a courtroom drama, dealt with everything from civil disobedience to euthanasia. Its father-and-son team of lawyers, unlike the other popular television lawyer Perry Mason, occasionally even lost a case.

East Side West Side (1963–1964) had a most unlikely television hero—a social worker, played by film star George C. Scott. This realistic series, filmed like *The Defenders,* in the mean streets of New York City, regularly exposed such social issues as racism, child abuse, and poverty. It made viewers think and offered no easy solutions. CBS had a hard time attracting sponsors to this controversial program, which was ahead of its time. Like other worthy dramatic series, *East Side West Side* was unable to convert its good reviews into a large viewing audience and lasted only a season.

Perhaps the most innovative drama series of the 1960s, however, was *The Fugitive* (1963–1967). Loosely based on the Victor Hugo novel *Les Misérables,* it was the story of Richard Kimble, a doctor wrongly accused and convicted of murdering his wife. Escaping en route to prison after his conviction, Kimble was on the run, trying to keep one step ahead of his dogged pursuer, Lieutenant Philip Gerard. Unlike most of the previous dramatic series, *The Fugitive* told a continuing story from episode to episode, as Kimble interacted with people that he met while on the run. In the final two-part episode, the real killer, the infamous "one-armed man," is finally exposed, and Kimble is cleared. It was the most watched single program of the decade.

Silly Sitcoms

Not all of the dramatic shows on television were of such high caliber. Many of the police and crime shows that replaced the westerns of the late 1950s and early 1960s were criticized as mindless and excessively violent.

Even more criticized were the decade's sitcoms. With a few exceptions, such as the wise and funny *Dick Van Dyke Show*, they were far below the quality of *I Love Lucy* and *The Honeymooners*. One major subgenre that established itself was rural comedies, harking back to a simpler, less troubled America. This new subject matter was first and best represented by *The Andy Griffith Show* (1960–1968). The title performer portrayed a homespun sheriff in the sleepy little North Carolina town of Mayberry. Comedian Don Knotts won five Emmys as Andy's goofy and bumbling deputy, Barney Fife. Far sillier was *The Beverly Hillbillies*, which debuted two years later. Condemned by the critics as childish, the show was about a family of mountain folk who strike it rich when they discover oil on their land and subsequently move to Southern California. Despite the less than enthusiastic critical response, *The Beverly Hillbillies* quickly became the number one program in the country, the first comedy series since *I Love Lucy* to achieve that distinction.

Another sitcom subgenre was fantasy shows. They included series about a talking horse (*Mr. Ed*), a lovely witch doubling as a housewife (*Bewitched*), a visiting extraterrestrial (*My Favorite Martian*), and a genie at the beck and call of a former astronaut (*I Dream of Jeannie*). Another form of escapism, these shows, all extremely popular in the mid- to late 1960s, took people's minds off the grim reality of the day—in particular the escalating war in Vietnam and the sharp division it was creating in American society.

The Living Room War

The Vietnam War, begun in 1957, was the longest armed conflict in which the United States has been involved. It began as an internal conflict in Southeast Asia when the Communist nation of North Vietnam attempted to take over democratic South Vietnam. The United States was afraid that if South Vietnam was forced to embrace communism, so would much of Southeast Asia, and it sent advisors and financial aid to South Vietnam. In 1965 the administration of Democratic president Lyndon Johnson began to send sizable numbers of ground troops to help the weakened, corrupt government of South Vietnam resist the invaders.

The television networks gave full coverage to the war, with correspondents reporting regularly from the front lines in Vietnam. For the first time in history, the American public saw a war, in all

THE VIETNAM WAR WAS THE FIRST ARMED CONFLICT THE UNITED STATES PARTICIPATED IN THAT WAS FULLY COVERED BY TELEVISION. ALTHOUGH TELEVISION COVERAGE WAS LARGELY SUPPORTIVE OF THE WAR AT FIRST, BY BRINGING THE FIGHTING INTO AMERICAN LIVING ROOMS, IT GAVE MOMENTUM TO THE ANTI-WAR EFFORT AS AMERICANS WERE INCREASINGLY SHOCKED AND DISCOURAGED BY WHAT THEY SAW.

its grim reality, firsthand. Television brought the war into people's homes, most significantly at the dinner hour on the evening news. The conflict quickly became known as America's "living room war."

At the start, the networks supported the war, as did most of the nation. But as the body count of American soldiers escalated and the war dragged on with no clear end in sight, millions of Americans began to doubt that the war could be won.

CBS's Walter Cronkite, the most respected newsman on television, questioned the military's strategy as far back as 1965, but largely remained neutral on the air. He traveled to Vietnam for his second visit to

PRESIDENT LYNDON JOHNSON WATCHES GRIMLY AS THE *SATURN I* ROCKET SOARS INTO SPACE. TELEVISION'S COVERAGE OF THE VIETNAM WAR HELPED TO DESTROY JOHNSON'S PRESIDENCY, AND HE LATER REFUSED TO RUN FOR ANOTHER TERM. THE AIDE TO JOHNSON'S FAR RIGHT IS PRESS SECRETARY BILL MOYERS, WHO WOULD BECOME ONE OF TELEVISON'S MOST RESPECTED JOURNALISTS AND COMMENTATORS.

the front in early 1968 soon after the Tet Offensive, when the Viet Cong, North Vietnam's pro-Communist forces, began an intense attack on South Vietnam's cities and towns. After his return, Cronkite hosted a half-hour special about the war. He closed the program with an un-precedented editorial. "For it seems now more certain than ever that the bloody experience of Vietnam is to end in a stalemate," he told the nation. "The only rational way out, then, will be to negotiate, not as vic-tors but as an honorable people who lived up to their pledge to defend democracy, and did the best they could."

Reportedly, President Johnson clicked off the set in the White House after the program and said to his aides, "If I've lost Cronkite, I've lost middle America." A little more than a month later, on March 31, 1968, Johnson went on television to make the surprise announcement that he would "not seek and [would] not accept" a nomination for a second full term as president.

The Vietnam War, however, did not end with the close of Johnson's presidency. Although a major withdrawal of U.S. troops began in 1969, the war dragged on until 1975. In that same year, South Vietnam fell to the North, and the nation became one, united political entity. All in all, about 58,000 Americans lost their lives in Vietnam.

Technological Advances

Television's extraordinary coverage of the war in Vietnam was just another indication of the medium's technological advances in the 1960s. The signal and picture quality were greatly improved, and there were more channels than ever before to choose from. Then, an act of Congress declared that all sets manufactured after April 30, 1964, must be capable of receiving stations numbered from fourteen to eighty-three on the dial, known as ultrahigh frequency (UHF) signal stations. "Booster" boxes and "rabbit ears," antennas placed on the top of television sets, became standard equipment and helped improve reception of the UHF station signals.

That same landmark year of 1964 saw such innovations as mobile cameras, slow-motion filming, and instant-replay capability transform television sports coverage. Suddenly television viewers had the best seat for watching sporting events right in their den or living room. Millions of fans stayed home to watch their favorite baseball, football, and basketball teams compete on television.

Sports shows, including ABC's innovative *Wide World of Sports*, a Saturday afternoon spectacle that debuted in April 1961, became big business and extremely profitable. The first Super Bowl game, televised at the end of the 1966–1967 football season, garnered a home-viewing audience of nearly 57 million, the biggest television audience for the sport up to that time. Since then, the Super Bowl has become an American institution and one of the biggest television events of the year.

Perhaps the greatest advance in television technology in the 1960s was the perfection of color television. After years of experimentation and development, color finally took off in the middle of the decade. By 1990, 98 percent of American households owned color television sets.

Color Television

THE TECHNOLOGY THAT PRODUCED COLOR TELEVISION WOULD QUICKLY MAKE THIS OLD BLACK-AND-WHITE SET WITH ITS RABBIT EARS ANTENNA OBSOLETE.

"If we let our imagination plunge ahead, we may . . . dream of television in faithful color," said RCA's David Sarnoff in 1927. That dream would become a reality in a surprisingly short time, but it would take decades for color television to be perfected and accepted by the networks and the general public.

Two years after Sarnoff's prophetic speech, Vladimir Zworykin received his first patent for a color television system. Meanwhile, CBS worked diligently on its own system. Its color-scanning disk, however, was incompatible with black-and-white receivers and was doomed from the start, despite a successful public demonstration in 1941. RCA, the owner of NBC, produced a color system compatible with black-and-white sets by 1949. The children's puppet show *Kukla, Fran and Ollie* became the first regularly scheduled program seen in color later that same year. In 1950 syndicator Frederic Ziv decided to film his western series *The Cisco Kid* in color, although it was seen on most sets in black and white. The industry thought Ziv was wasting his money, but *The Cisco Kid* remained a profitable series for years in reruns for the simple reason that it was the only filmed series of its time broadcast in color.

Another western, NBC's *Bonanza*, became the first major network series filmed in color in 1959. NBC unveiled its colorful peacock logo and became the "color network." Not until the next decade, however, would the other networks commit fully to broadcasting in color. By 1972 sales of color sets surpassed black-and-white sets for the first time. "In living color" was no longer a novelty, but the standard for all television broadcasting.

Television Conquers Space

When President Kennedy boldly announced, in 1961, his plan to put a man on the moon by the end of the decade, it seemed a distant or unattainable dream.

By then the "race for space" was well under way. The Soviet Union had sent cosmonaut Yuri Gagarin into space in April 1961. The United States' Mercury program launched three manned space flights over the next year and a half, climaxing in astronaut John Glenn orbiting the Earth in his space capsule *Friendship 7* on February 20, 1962. All three of these launches were covered by television and watched by millions of Americans at home, school, and work.

As manned space launches became more common, however, television viewership and coverage fell off. But when Kennedy's dream finally became a reality, it was a truly historic event. On July 16, 1969, the spacecraft *Apollo 11* blasted off from Cape Kennedy in Florida with three astronauts on board—Neil Armstrong, Edwin Aldrin, and Michael Collins. Each network had its own special studio set up in New York to cover the event at a combined cost of $13 million. Walter Cronkite, the anchorman most enthusiastic about space travel, was on the air for most of the thirty hours of live coverage. When Armstrong took his first steps on the lunar surface on July 20, 130 million Americans were watching, one of the biggest audiences in television history. "That's one small step for a man, one giant leap for mankind," Armstrong said as he walked on the moon. Back home on Earth, Cronkite appeared as awestruck as any viewer when he said, "It was as if you could have stood on the dock and waved goodbye to Columbus."

Television and the world had truly entered a new era of enhanced communications. The moon landing had ended a turbulent decade on a resounding note of optimism. Television had recorded America at its best and its worst. Satellites had beamed major events to the world. Television had transformed a vast planet into a global village where news of an event in one place would be almost instantaneously sent to every other corner of the world. This global village would grow and become even more dependent on television in the decades to come.

TELEVISION COMES TO THE REMOTE SWEDISH VILLAGE OF KAALASLUSPA IN LAPLAND IN 1962. BY THE 1970S, TELEVISION HAD BROUGHT THE WORLD CLOSER TOGETHER THAN EVER BEFORE.

SIX

Expanding Choices

For its first quarter century, commercial television developed and grew, but always within the confines of the three major networks—CBS, NBC, and ABC. In the 1970s, that trend began to change. PBS became a creative force in television with a variety of cultural and news programs that drew millions of new viewers. Time, Incorporated, the communications and entertainment conglomerate, began the first premier cable channel, Home Box Office (HBO), in 1972. It would be only the first of many new channels sent directly to a household via cable wires as opposed to broadcasting waves received by an antenna. This new format would eventually challenge commercial television's supremacy on the airwaves.

The Birth of Cable Television

Cable television was not a new idea in the 1970s. In June 1948 John Watson became one of the first cable providers when he strung two wires from a pole to his warehouse so he could get reception for his store's demonstration models. Television reception from Philadelphia stations had been previously blocked by mountains. While connecting his store, Watson "wired" eight local homes whose reception was also hindered by the mountains. In doing so, the first cable system came into being.

By 1958 small cable companies served a modest total of 450 subscribers in numerous states. In the 1960s, TelePrompTer emerged as the major cable provider in the United States. By then cable systems used microwaves, an intense form of electromagnetic radiation, to transmit programming to cable wires that then relayed them to individual customers. Microwaves, unlike the traditional radio waves used to transmit television signals, could carry more information and be sent directly from one specific location to another.

Cable's growth through the 1970s was slow but steady. Nearly ever year a new technological development increased its power and capability. In 1973 HBO and two other cable systems aired the first satellite-delivered programs to households in the United States. The companies discovered that satellites from space were a cheaper and more efficient way of transmitting programs to cable customers than microwaves. In 1975 HBO's satellite transmission of the Muhammad Ali-Joe Frazier heavyweight boxing match, known as the "Thrilla in Manila," was a groundbreaking broadcast. "It crossed cable over the demarcation line from a distant regional service to a programming service," said pioneering cable lawyer Jack Cole. Cable television was finding its niche and could no longer be ignored by the commercial networks.

The Sitcom's Golden Age

For most of the 1970s, however, the established networks still reigned supreme. Many of their sitcoms broke new ground, reflecting the real world in ways few television shows had done before. *The Mary Tyler Moore Show* (1970–1977) centered on a single woman in her thirties who was the assistant news producer at a television station in Minneapolis, Minnesota. The experiences faced by Mary Richards, the character Mary Tyler Moore portrayed, reflected the lives of millions of American career women, many of whom led fulfilling lives, outside the bounds of marriage and family. The show was also a clever satire of television news, especially in the vain, preening character of news anchorman Ted Baxter. *MTM* was so successful in

Ted Turner— Cable Television Pioneer

In 1963 Ted Turner was a twenty-four-year-old running his late father's billboard advertising company. A maverick who believed in taking risks to reach success, Turner decided to diversify his business. Against the advice of his friends and colleagues, he bought two failing television stations in Atlanta, Georgia. Through clever advertising and by airing the games of the Atlanta Braves baseball and Atlanta Hawks hockey teams (both of which he subsequently bought), he made his stations profitable.

In 1976 Turner again defied conventional wisdom and decided to join the growing ranks of cable stations by beaming the signal from one of his Atlanta stations to a satellite. As a result, WTBS (Turner Broadcasting System) became the world's first "superstation." In just two years it was reaching two million viewers across the country.

Turner's next move proved to be his biggest gamble yet. Knowing viewers' voracious appetite for news, he launched the first twenty-four-hour all-news network, Cable News Network (CNN) in 1980. Critics predicted it would fail, but CNN quickly became so successful that Turner launched a second all-news service, CNN Headline News, less than two years later.

At about the same time, Turner bought up MGM Studio's film library of more than three thousand old movies for about $1 billion. In 1994 he started Turner Classic Movies (TCM), which regularly airs these and other old films.

Turner merged his media empire in 1996 with Time Warner, the largest entertainment conglomerate in the world, and became a vice chairman of the corporation, a position he held until 2003. Today, Ted Turner is one of the richest men in America, his wealth built on the idea that cable television can provide viewers with fare they cannot get on commercial television.

IN A CLASSIC EPISODE OF *ALL IN THE FAMILY*, ENTERTAINER SAMMY DAVIS JR. PAYS A VISIT TO THE BUNKER HOUSEHOLD AND IN ONE OF THE FUNNIEST MOMENTS IN 1970S TELEVISION, PLANTS A KISS ON THE LIPS OF RACIST ARCHIE BUNKER.

its seven-year run that it sired three successful spin-offs, including the dramatic series *Lou Grant* about life in the newsroom of a major daily newspaper.

M*A*S*H (1972–1983) was based on a hit movie about a group of Army medics during the Korean War. It was an unusual sitcom in that it dealt seriously with issues of war at a time when Americans were questioning their country's involvement in another conflict, the Vietnam War that ended in 1975.

Social issues were central to a group of series produced by Norman Lear in the early 1970s. The first and most controversial of them was *All in the Family* (1971–1983), whose central character—working-class husband and father Archie Bunker—was an overt, unapologetic bigot. Lear and Carroll O'Connor, the liberal actor who portrayed Archie, insisted that the show was exposing and condemning Bunker's bigotry through humor. But some viewers made the character into a folk hero admired for his outspoken stance on race, politics, and other sensitive issues.

Archie's bigotry was balanced by a spin-off series *Maude,* about his wife's upper-middle-class liberal cousin. Then, spun off from *Maude* was the series *Good Times* about Maude's black maid, Florida, and her family who lived on Chicago's South Side. Another Lear sitcom with African Americans as its primary focus was *The Jeffersons,* which had a father figure who was as prejudiced against whites as Archie Bunker was against blacks.

NBC's greatest contribution to comedy in this new era of social awareness was *Saturday Night Live,* a ninety-minute late night comedy-variety show that debuted in October 1975. Shot live in New York, the show's wild and irreverent sketch-comedy format, which included a weekly spoof of the news, was a runaway hit and is still popular with viewers today. It introduced a fresh group of young comic actors, many of who went on to become stars of prime-time television shows and feature films. They included Chevy Chase, John Belushi, and Gilda Radner and in later years, Dan Ackroyd, Billy Crystal, Eddie Murphy, and Will Ferrell.

Television Movies

Dramatic series of the era tended to look to the past and not to the present realities gripping the American scene. Among the most popular series were the Depression-era family drama *The Waltons* (1972–1981) and the 1870s midwestern family drama *Little House on the Prairie* (1974–1983). Both these shows laced their drama with sentimentality. More contemporary and hard-hitting were such urban crime shows as *Kojak* (1973–1978) that featured a bald-headed police lieutenant who liked lollipops. Some of these police dramas were well written and acted, but others such as *Starsky and Hutch* (1975–1979) had simplistic plots, lots of action, and were increasingly criticized for excessive violence.

While movies had been a television staple since the beginnings of regular broadcasting, there had been no movies (ninety minutes or

The Mini-Series

An outgrowth of the made-for-television movie is the mini-series, which as its name implies tells a dramatic story in two-hour prime-time segments parceled out over several nights or weeks. Many of the most popular mini-series were based on best-selling, often epic novels, such as *Shogun*; *Rich Man, Poor Man*; and *The Thorn Birds*.

The most watched and most critically acclaimed mini-series was *Roots*, based on author Alex Haley's fictionalized saga of his African-American family from 1750 to the American Civil War. *Roots* ran for eight consecutive nights in prime time in January 1977. The final episode was watched by an estimated 100 million viewers, more than any previous program in television history. The show not only brought about a major reevaluation of slavery in America and a renewed interest in black history in general, but also set off a national mania for genealogy, not just among black Americans but people of all racial and ethnic backgrounds.

The mini-series, as a genre, lost its popularity in the 1980s, as producers found them too costly to produce and too much of a ratings' gamble. However, in 1989 the popularity of the eight-hour adaptation of Larry McMurty's Pulitzer Prize–winning western novel *Lonesome Dove* renewed interest in this respected dramatic format.

longer) made specifically for television until the mid-1960s. While these early made-for-television movies tended to be pilots for new series, by the early 1970s, they focused more on serious issues that were rarely, if ever, considered in Hollywood movies. *A Case of Rape* (1974) dealt with this little-discussed crime against women. *That Certain Summer* (1972) explored homosexuality, while *Brian's Song* (1971) examined the early death from disease of real-life football player Brian Piccolo. These and other television movies dealt with often controversial or overlooked subjects with sensitivity and intelligence.

Television movies were also a popular training ground for new directors. *Duel* (1971), a harrowing tale about a commuter pursued on the roadways by a maniacal truck driver, was the first feature-length film directed by Steven Spielberg.

Today some television movies continue this fine tradition of high-quality entertainment. But others are merely exploitative or sensationalistic. When Amy Fisher, dubbed the "Long Island Lolita," was arrested after shooting her lover's wife in 1992, all three networks rushed out their made-for-television movies about the much publicized crime.

The Watergate Hearings

As engrossing as any made-for-television movie or mini-series were the congressional hearings into the Watergate scandal of 1973–1974. It all began on June 17, 1972, when a group of men was arrested for breaking into the Democratic Party headquarters in the Watergate apartment and office building

THE WATERGATE HEARINGS INTO THE NIXON WHITE HOUSE MADE FOR UNFORGETTABLE TELEVISION VIEWING. IN THE END, THE HEARINGS AND THEIR AFTERMATH LEFT A STAIN ON THE NIXON PRESIDENCY AND BROUGHT ABOUT THE RESIGNATION, IN AUGUST 1974, OF THE EMBATTLED LEADER.

in Washington, D.C. The incident was all but forgotten in the days leading up to the presidential election that November, which President Richard Nixon won in a landslide. But investigative reporters from *The Washington Post* uncovered a link between the burglars and the Nixon White House and a subsequent coverup to hide that connection.

In February 1973, the Senate voted to establish a committee to investigate the affair. The Senate hearings began on May 17 and were covered live each day by PBS. They were then rebroadcast on tape each night. The hearings proved riveting viewing, and PBS stations received their highest ratings since the network had been founded. The three commercial networks also carried the hearings on a rotating basis and attracted a large viewing audience as well.

Through the summer of 1973, up to 85 percent of American households watched part or all of the hearings. A gallery of colorful characters, as unforgettable as those on any fictional series, took center stage in this real-life drama. They included Senator Sam Ervin, the folksy but determined chairman of the Senate committee; presidential counsel John Dean who first revealed Nixon's role in the coverup; and the loyal, ex-Army artillery man and FBI agent G. Gordon Liddy, a mastermind of the burglary who refused to incriminate the president. (Liddy's 1982 autobiography was later made into a television movie, and he has since become a syndicated radio talk host.)

One by one, Nixon aides were indicted for conspiracy and other charges in the Watergate scandal and served time in prison. Nixon's popularity in the polls plummeted, and the outcry for his impeachment grew. Finally, appearing composed and calm before an international television audience on August 8, 1974, Nixon announced that the next day he would resign the presidency—the first U.S. president to ever do so. As author Joe Garner has pointed out, Nixon had used television back in 1952 to save his political career when he delivered a skilful speech denying he had taken illegal funds when he was a senator. "Twenty-two years later," wrote Garner, "television was there to chronicle his political self-destruction."

The Video Revolution

Videotape, cheaper and easier to use than film, had been the standard for recording and broadcasting television programs since it was first used on a CBS News telecast in November 1956. That same year, the first practical, commercially produced video tape recorder (VTR) was released by Ampex. It cost $50,000. This ancestor of the videocassette recorder (VCR) resembled an audio tape recorder with large spools over which magnetic tape passed at high speeds.

A cheaper VTR for home use was put out by Sony in 1964. When connected to the family television set, it could record one hour of television programming. Only a few hundred sold. It was not until the fall of 1977 that an inexpensive VCR that used today's familiar VHS videotape cassettes appeared on the American market. Within a few years, the

VIDEO RECORDING WAS STILL IN ITS INFANCY IN 1962 WHEN THIS WESTINGHOUSE "VIDICON" FIRST HIT THE MARKET. BY THE LATE 1970S, VIDEOTAPING HAD CHANGED THE WAY MANY PEOPLE VIEWED TELEVISION.

VCR became standard equipment in most American households.

VCRs and videocassettes revolutionized American television viewing. Now viewers could set the timer on their VCRs and record a favorite program when they were away from home, asleep, or watching another show. Even better, when they sat down to watch the program that they had recorded earlier, they could use the VCR remote to fast-forward past all the commercials.

Another growing use for VCRs was watching prerecorded movies, which first started appearing on the market in 1980. Within a few years, video rental stores were popping up across the country. Video and computer games, often requiring their own equipment, were further turning the television set into a complete entertainment center that family members could use in multiple ways.

Groundbreaking Programs

And what were viewers of the early 1980s taping with their newly purchased VCRs? The hottest new network show of 1981 was a groundbreaking hour-long drama called *Hill Street Blues*. It was a cop show unlike any that had come before it. In an unprecedented move, NBC gave producer Steven Bochco and his partner Michael Kozoll total artistic control over the series. *Hill Street Blues* had an extraordinarily large cast of characters, mostly played by experienced but little-known actors. The precinct was set in a large decaying urban neighborhood in an unnamed city and the scripts and cinematography were exceptionally gritty and realistic, setting a new standard for acceptable language, violence, and sexual content. Plots and crimes were rarely neatly tied up in one episode, but often spread over several installments or more. Like a novel, the show presented three or more subplots developing at the same time.

Hill Street Blues, which ran through 1987, won an unprecedented eight Emmy Awards in its first season and set the blueprint for such future Bochco hit dramatic series as *L.A. Law* (1986–1994) and *NYPD Blue* (1993–2005), as well as non-Bochco shows such as the medical series *ER* (1994–), the most successful dramatic series of the last decade.

THE LONG-TERM EFFECTS OF TELEVISION ON CHILDREN WERE BECOMING A MAJOR CONCERN BY THE 1980S. VIOLENCE, SEX, AND COMMERCIALISM WERE ALL SEEN AS NEGATIVE INFLUENCES ON A GENERATION RAISED ON TELEVISION.

More traditional, but just as popular, was *The Cosby Show* (1984–1992), the most popular sitcom of the 1980s. Comedian and actor Bill Cosby had been the first black actor to star in a dramatic series in the 1960s show *I Spy*. He created *The Cosby Show* not only to combat the violence, sex, and exploitation that he believed was overrunning television in the early 1980s but as a vehicle to present his own ideas on education and child rearing. He also wanted to create a comedy about an upper-middle-class black family, the Huxtables, rarely seen before on television. Race was not a major issue in the Huxtable household; the problems faced by the parents and children were ones that many American families could identify with.

Cable Comes into Its Own

While network television continued to enjoy wide viewership in the 1980s, its dominance of the airwaves was gone forever. By 1989, 60 percent of American households had cable, while prime-time network viewership by that year had fallen from 80 percent to 68 percent. HBO and the Turner-owned stations were joined by a myriad of new cable stations, many of them appealing to a special niche of the viewing audience or dealing with a particular theme or subject. Whatever their interest, viewers could find a station that catered to it. The days when the entire family gathered around the set to watch *The Ed Sullivan Show*, the most democratic of variety shows, had become as obsolete as rabbit ears and housetop antennas.

The number of television sets in a household multiplied as each family member wanted to watch his or her own programs. Grandpa might tune into the History Channel to watch a show about World War II, while Grandma watches an old movie musical on American Movie Classics or Turner Classic Movies. Sports-minded Dad can tune in a game almost any hour of the day on ESPN and take a break to catch up on the latest news on CNN or NBC's MSNBC. Mom can get new home decorating ideas on the Home and Garden Channel or see what tomorrow's weather will be like on the Weather Channel. The teenagers in the house can enjoy the latest music videos of their favorite artists on MTV (Music Television), as the younger children watch programs targeting their age group on Nickelodeon, The Disney Channel, or Cartoon Network. And these are just a few of the most popular cable channels out of the hundreds currently available through more advanced cable systems. The network stations are included in the cable package as well as HBO, Showtime, and a dozen or more other movie or special-interest channels that viewers pay a premium to watch.

Could television get any more advanced? As new technology and programming in the last decade and a half have shown, the answer is a resounding "yes."

ONCE LIMITED TO RURAL HOUSEHOLDS THAT COULD NOT GET REGULAR TELEVISION RECEPTION, CABLE TELEVISION HAD BECOME A NECESSITY FOR MILLIONS OF AMERICANS BY THE 1990s.

SEVEN

Digital and Beyond

In 1993 cable television entered a new world of diversification. Cable that previously brought only television signals into the home could now be combined with Internet service that was up to one thousand times faster than the copper wiring used by the telephone company for dial-up access to the Internet. Ever more amazing, cable was able to provide telecommunications as well. By the start of the twenty-first century, cable companies were providing Internet for millions of households and a growing number were using cable for their home telephone service.

Cable Grows Up

Through the 1980s, premium cable networks such as HBO and Showtime had been known mostly for showing first-run movies, comedy specials, and sports events that viewers could not see on commercial television. In the 1990s, these channels, especially HBO, began creating more original programming. They took advantage of the fact that as premium channels, they were not under the regulations of the FCC and had few restrictions in their use of language, violence, and sexual material.

The Larry Sanders Show (1992–1998), a behind-the-scenes look at a late night talk show, revealed the underside of show business with satirical bite. *Sex and the City* (1998–2004) was a frank, often comic

Television—
Not Just for Broadcasting

Television technology does not only exist to bring entertainment into homes. It has some other important uses in our world.

Hospitals and other health-care facilities use television monitors to show a fetus's progress in a mother's womb, trace the colon in a colonoscopy or serve as a visual aid to a surgeon during surgery.

Explorers and scientists use television cameras in undersea craft to study the bottom of the deepest oceans or in satellites to examine the depths of outer space.

We have all had the dubious honor of being watched on a surveillance camera. These cameras are used in hotel lobbies, stores, school halls, and other public places to deter criminal activity and to help security guards and police officers see a crime in progress and catch the perpetrators.

Television can also be used as a means to transmit textual information. Teletext makes textual data—news, sports, weather, and other information—available to viewers with decoders. This service is popular in Europe and the United Kingdom, but has to date met with little success in the United States.

look, at the lives of four single career women living in Manhattan. The most popular and groundbreaking drama on HBO, however, was *The Sopranos*, which debuted in 1999. This intimate view of the private and public lives of a Mafia family became a national phenomenon during its seven seasons and is, to date, the most successful series in cable history. It spawned a host of similar dramas on HBO that mixed comedy and drama to a degree rarely seen on television before.

New Networks

Not all the innovative programming in the 1990s was coming from cable. In 1987 Fox Broadcasting Company, part of Australian Rupert Murdoch's media empire, launched the Fox Network, broadcast to 180 stations nationwide. It was the first serious commercial competition the three major networks faced since Du Mont went off the air in 1955. From the start, Fox set out to draw in younger viewers with wild, irreverent programming. *Married . . . with Children* (1987–1997) was a sitcom about a totally dysfunctional family held together more by dislike than love. Despite critical disapproval, it became a huge hit.

The Simpsons (1989–), is about another daffy family, this time animated. Irreverent in its attitude toward American values and social issues, *The Simpsons* is the longest-running sitcom and animated series in television history.

Fox proved it had the muscle to go up against the "Big Three" when in 1994 it outbid CBS for rights to broadcast National Conference games of the National Football League (NFL). Many sports fans tuned in to Fox for the first time and stayed to watch other shows.

WITH HUNDREDS OF NETWORKS AND CHANNELS TO CHOOSE FROM, TELEVISION VIEWERS OFTEN FIND THEMSELVES SURFING THE DIAL WITH THEIR TRUSTY REMOTE CONTROL.

Fox's phenomenal success led to the start of two other new networks in the 1990s—United Paramount Network (UPN) and the WB Television Network—both backed by major media conglomerates. While each has had success appealing to audiences of women, African Americans, and teenagers, neither has enjoyed the success of Fox.

A Technological Explosion

Just when it looked like television technology had gone as far as it could, there were new and exciting developments. By 1979 Japanese technicians were developing an experimental new system of what has come to be called high-definition television (HDTV). As its name implies, HDTV provides viewers with a much clearer and concise picture image through an increase in the number of scanning lines per frame

HIGH-DEFINITION TELEVISION (HDTV) IS AMONG THE NEWEST TRENDS IN TECHNOLOGY. THIS TECHNICIAN IS INSPECTING SCREENS BEFORE THEY ARE SOLD.

and the number of pixels, the tiny areas of illumination of which an image on the screen is composed. Today, the best HD televisions can display up to two million pixels, creating nearly ten times the resolution of an ordinary television set.

By the early 1990s, the Japanese had a fully functioning commercial HD system. The United States was anxious to catch up and developed its own HDTV system based on digital images. These are images created by computers using data translated into a series of binary numbers. All earlier television systems, including the first Japanese HDTV, were based on analog, in which data is represented by measurable physical quantities, not computer code. The first public HDTV broadcast in the United States was the launching of the space shuttle *Discovery* in October 1998.

Eager to set new and higher standards for broadcasting, the FCC originally decreed that all commercial television broadcasts must be in digital format by 2007. Since then, due to difficulties in manufacturing and other economic factors, that deadline has been extended to somewhere between 2010 and 2015. By 2005 all of the major television networks broadcast nearly their entire prime-time schedules in HDTV, but only about 18 million HD television sets were then in use. By 2006 this number is expected to triple. In the meantime, all existing analog television sets must have a special adapter to receive broadcasts in high definition.

While the quality of television images is improving, new ways of transmitting them have also been developed. In the last decade, satellite television has gone from being a novelty to a competitive alternative to cable.

As its name suggests, satellite television is broadcast via telecommunications satellites hovering about 22,000 miles (35,406 kilometers) above Earth. Unlike cable systems, which use satellites to receive broadcasts that are then sent through cable wires, the signal from the satellites is sent directly to customers who subscribe to the service. The signals cover a wide range of the Earth's surface and are not obstructed by mountains and tall buildings that often block regular radio wave transmissions. Furthermore, the satellites move with the Earth's shifting orbit, so the signal remains constant and in the same relationship with the location it is beamed to.

With satellite television, the various station signals are received at a broadcast center, which then beams the signals to one or more satellites in space. The satellite receives the signal and rebroadcasts it back to Earth, where it is received by a small satellite dish attached to the roof or outside a subscriber's home or apartment. The dish relays the signal to a receiver inside that then processes it so it can be transmitted to the television set and then broadcast on the screen.

In the early 1990s, satellite television companies appealed primarily to consumers living in rural areas beyond the range of broadcast television or where cable companies had not yet ventured. Today, many consumers in other areas are choosing direct broadcast satellite television as a worthwhile alternative to cable. In November 1999 President Bill Clinton signed the Satellite Home Viewer Improvement Act (SHVIA) into law, allowing consumers to receive broadcast signals from direct satellite systems and expanding Americans' choices for television reception. In 2005 one provider alone, EchoStar Communications, had more than eleven million subscribers.

The Future of Television

What is next for television? Perhaps shifting the medium to other outlets, such as the home computer. In the 2000s, more and more Americans were watching video clips and even longer programs on their computers via the Internet. In 2005 about 53 percent of Internet-equipped households used high-speed, broadband Internet access, greatly improving the speed of their video reception. A number of Internet servers are increasing their capability for video. Yahoo!, for instance, has added video clips from CNN, ABC News, the Associated Press (AP), and National Public Radio (NPR) to its news site. In July 2005, five million

THIS COMMUNICATIONS TOWER IS PART OF THE SATELLITE TELEVISION SYSTEM THAT HAS BECOME THE NUMBER-ONE RIVAL TO CABLE IN THE TWENTY-FIRST CENTURY.

Plasma Television

Imagine fifty years ago that someone told Philo Farnsworth that one day his television would hang from the wall like a piece of art and produce a clear, perfect picture from a flat, wide screen. Although a visionary inventor, Farnsworth may not have believed it. But today, this kind of television, called plasma television, is a reality.

Plasma is a gas composed of ions, electrically charged atoms, and electrons, which are negatively charged particles. When the electrons of the television signal hit the plasma atoms, the collisions cause a release of energy in the form of light. The light energy then causes the phosphorous material in the pixels to give off light. The pixels have areas of red, green, and blue that combine in different groupings to produce a picture that can contain nearly every color in the light spectrum.

Plasma television has several advantages over the traditional cathode-ray tube that has been standard on television sets for seventy-five years. Because there is no tube, the set has about one-fourth the depth of the traditional set, about 6 inches (15.2 centimeters), and weighs about half as much. Thus, it can be easily hung on a wall. Because it is flat, the plasma set can be seen from virtually any place in a room. A plasma television is a flexible monitor that can be used for everything from a home video receiver to a computer screen. Finally, it has a longer life span than most traditional televisions, about 30,000 hours. The day may not be far off when most American households have a "hanging" television.

viewers watched America Online's (AOL's) live Webcast of the Live 8 Concert series. Viewers were able to switch from one live concert to another, something they could not do on regular television. Internet watchers can also interact with the media and access archives in an instant.

The cable and commercial networks have been turning their attention to Internet capabilities as well. Nickelodeon Network, MTV Networks, and CNN have all started their own Internet services. MTV Overdrive has been called by *The New York Times* "the slickest attempt yet to combine the performance of television with the interactivity of

TELEVISION OF THE FUTURE MAY BE WATCHED BY MORE PEOPLE ON THE INTERNET THAN ON TRADITIONAL SETS. THIS INTERNET USER IS WATCHING A LIVE "WEBCAST" OF RUSSIAN PRESIDENT VLADIMIR PUTIN BEING INTERVIEWED FROM MOSCOW.

the Internet." Even CBS now offers video news updates and news features that supplement its thirty-minute evening television newscast.

Is the day far off when the person looking for entertainment and information will find it all in the click of a mouse rather than a television remote? Whether on a cathode-ray tube, a plasma set, or a computer, the viewer of the near future may find his or her choices expanding to more than five hundred channels, broadcast in full stereo sound piped in through a virtual-reality helmet that will give new meaning to the old NBC slogan "in living color."

Wasteland or Paradise?

Will the television programming of tomorrow keep pace with these technological marvels?

Many television critics see the rise and predominance of reality television as the return of "the vast wasteland" that Newton Minow warned of in the early 1960s. Shows such as *Survivor* (2000–) and *The Apprentice* (2004–) pit real people against one another for a chance at fame and riches. Critics say these shows display humankind at its worst.

Even more foreboding is the influence of entertainment television on television news. While the CBS newsmagazine *60 Minutes* continues to produce high quality telejournalism, many of television's newsmagazines have become the video equivalent of the newspaper tabloid, concentrating on celebrity interviews and gossip, true crime stories, and anything that will titillate viewers. High-profile criminal cases—such as former football player O. J. Simpson's trial for the murder of his wife and her friend in 1995 and the Michael Jackson child abuse trial of 2005—have dominated the medium and made Court TV, another cable niche channel, at times one of the most popular on the dial.

Will tomorrow's television be a wasteland or a paradise? Will it be a positive force for change or a passive and irresponsible escape tool? Based on present evidence, the potential exists for both scenarios. Economically, television is the greatest selling tool in human history. Every

SENSATIONALISM SEEMED TO REACH A FEVERISH PEAK WITH THE INTENSE TELEVISION COVERAGE OF THE O. J. SIMPSON TRIAL IN 1995. THIS MEDIA FRENZY TOOK PLACE OUTSIDE THE COURTROOM WHILE THE TRIAL WAS IN SESSION.

day we are bombarded with hundreds of commercials for every kind of product and service. Television advertising may manipulate and mislead us at times, if we do not view it with a critical eye. At the same time, advertising helps drive and stimulate national economies in addition to paying the bills for commercial programming. It is hard to imagine the global marketplace without it.

Just as television can sell products, it can sell political candidates and their agendas. Since the Kennedy-Nixon debates of 1960, television has been the single most powerful tool used to sway voters during campaigns and elections. Presidents and politicians can use the power of television to persuade, manipulate, and even divide the public. Then again, political leaders can use the medium just as easily and effectively to unite us in troubled times, such as in the aftermath of the terrorist attacks of September 11, 2001. Television, a visual medium, tends to simplify complicated issues and emphasize the surface at the cost of substance. However, television can also deliver news and investigate issues in depth and with maximum emotional impact. Television can be a window to the world and its problems and can serve as a conduit for the intelligent discussion and debate of issues.

Finally, television's impact on society in general has been tremendous. We have been told time and again that most of us watch too much television. Some believe that such a passive activity is turning us into a nation of couch potatoes who run the risk of becoming physically unfit and mentally lazy. The greatest concern has been for children who, according to one recent survey, watch an average of twenty-five hours of television each week. Some studies have found evidence that too much television affects a child's performance in school and slows the maturing process, dependent on social interaction. However, other experts claim that television viewing, in moderation, can sharpen our social skills, widen our worldview, and intellectually challenge us with dramatic programming that is as multidimensional and complex in its plotting as a good novel.

After seventy-five years, television—for good or bad—has now earned a permanent place in our culture. Its history has been recorded in

DRAMATIC PROOF OF HOW FAR TELEVISION HAS COME IN ABOUT SEVENTY-FIVE YEARS. ABOVE IS AN IMAGE OF A WOMAN IN THE 1930S FROM JOHN LOGIE BAIRD'S THIRTY-LINE TELEVISION. COMPARE THIS TO (ON THE FOLLOWING PAGE) . . .

. . . TODAY'S 45-INCH (114.3-CENTIMETER) FLAT SCREEN DISPLAY IN TOKYO, JAPAN. IT REPRODUCES IMAGES USING 6.22 MILLION PIXEL DOTS.

books and celebrated in television specials. Digital videodisks (DVDs) and archival museums have been devoted to the television of the past and present. Artifacts of this vibrant industry have been enshrined at the Smithsonian Institution's National Museum of American History in Washington, D.C.

Television's influence on our lives is enormous and will only continue to grow in the years and decades ahead. We, as consumers and creators, need to take it seriously and see that its influence is a positive force for humankind's entertainment and enlightenment. Happy viewing.

American Broadcasting Company (ABC)—A television network founded in 1943.

analog—Television transmission based on the representation of measurable units, not computerized symbols.

British Broadcasting Company (BBC)—A government-funded British television network founded in 1926.

cable television—A method of transmitting television signals in packages by satellite to cable systems that redistribute the programs through wires to individual households that pay for the service.

cathode-ray tube—A glass tube containing electrodes that glows fluorescent when connected to a source of electrical energy.

Columbia Broadcasting System (CBS)—A television network founded in 1927.

digital television—Television transmission in which images are created by the use of computerized symbols in a numerical binary form.

digital video disc (DVD)—A high-density compact disc for storing movies and other data.

Federal Communications Commission (FCC)—A government agency that regulates television and radio, founded in 1934.

high-definition television (HDTV)—A system of television that uses twice the standard number of scanning lines per frame to create a clearer, more detailed picture.

Home Box Office (HBO)—The first premium cable network founded in 1972.

kinescope—In the early days of television, a film made of a program, recorded from a television screen, that was then air mailed to other stations to be rebroadcast.

microwave—An intense form of electromagnetic radiation that can carry more information than radio waves and can be sent directly from one location to another.

mini-series—A filmed dramatic program that is broadcast over several or more evenings with a total running time of usually eight or more hours.

National Broadcasting Company (NBC)—A television network founded by RCA in 1926.

Nipkow Disk—An early transmitting system that sends images using a scanning disk, first conceived by Paul Gottlieb Nipkow in 1884.

pixel—The tiny areas of illumination of which an image on a television screen is composed.

Public Broadcasting Service (PBS)—A government- and publicly funded television network established in 1967 that features quality cultural, political, and educational programming often not available on the commercial networks.

rabbit ears—A two-pronged television antenna placed on top of a television set to help pull in broadcasting signals.

satellite television—A method of transmitting television using telecommunication satellites in space that rebroadcast television signals back to Earth and directly to households.

selenium—A nonmetallic element discovered in 1817 that is capable of transforming light into electrical signals, important in the early development of television.

situation comedy (sitcom)—A television genre, usually appearing in a half-hour format, that has long been a programming staple.

soap opera—A daily daytime television drama, usually centered on contemporary relationships, with a continuing story line.

ultrahigh frequency (UHF)—A band of radio frequencies that are received on channels ranging from fourteen to eighty-three on the television dial.

very high frequency (VHF)—A band of radio frequencies that are received on channels two to thirteen on the television dial.

videocassette recorder (VCR)—An electronic recorder capable of playing prerecorded videotapes and recording programs from television on tape; popular since the late 1970s.

Time Line

1817 Swedish chemist Jons Jacob Berzelius discovers the element selenium that will lead to the development of television.

1877 American inventor G. R. Carey conceives the first primitive television composed of selenium cells and electric lightbulbs.

1884 German inventor Paul Gottlieb Nipkow files a patent for a scanning disk transmitter, later called the Nipkow Disk.

1897 German physicist K. F. Braun invents the cathode-ray oscilloscope.

1902 Russian professor Boris Rosing experiments with transmitting and receiving images using the cathode tube.

1907 The word *television* first appears in print in an issue of *Scientific American.*

1914–1918 World War I brings most television research and development to a halt.

1918 English inventor A. A. Campbell Swinton conceives of the first all-electronic television system for sending and receiving images.

1923 Russian émigré Vladimir Zworykin patents the iconoscope, an electronic scanning transmitter.

1925 Scottish engineer John Logie Baird makes the first transmission of a moving image with his mechanical system.

1926 The Radio Corporation of American (RCA) founds the National Broadcasting Company (NBC).

1927 American Philo Farnsworth patents his improved cathode-ray tube, which he calls a "dissector."

1928 The General Electric Company (GE) opens the first experimental television station, WGY, in Schenectady, New York.

1929 Zworykin develops an improved cathode-ray picture tube called the kinescope; the British Broadcasting Company (BBC) adopts Baird's mechanical system and begins regular television broadcasts.

1930 NBC opens its first experimental television station, W2XBS, in New York City.

1932 W2XBS and CBS's W2XAB cover the November presidential election won by Franklin D. Roosevelt.

1934 The Federal Communications Commission (FCC) is founded to regulate radio and television.

1936 The BBC switches from a mechanical to an electronic television system.

1939 Television is a hit at the New York world's fair, which opens in April; soon after, RCA begins to produce and market its first commercial television sets.

1941 On April 30, the FCC authorizes unrestricted commercial television; NBC's W2XBS becomes WNBT, the nation's first commercial station.

1942–1945 Nearly all commercial broadcasting is suspended during the United States' involvement in World War II.

1946 Regular broadcasting resume on the three networks; RCA unveils its new television set, the 630; The Academy of Television Arts and Sciences is founded.

1947 In December, *The Howdy Doody Show*, the first network children's program, premieres on NBC.

1948 *Texaco Star Theater*, starring Milton Berle, debuts on NBC in September and becomes America's number one program.

1949 On January 25, the first Emmy Awards are presented in Los Angeles, California.

1951 On September 4, President Harry Truman addresses the opening of the Japanese Peace Treaty Conference in San Francisco, the first coast-to-coast television broadcast; *I Love Lucy* debuts on October 15.

1952 *Today*, the first early morning network program, debuts in NBC; the first issue of *TV Guide* goes on sale.

1953 *Tonight!*, a late night variety/talk show hosted by Steve Allen, goes on the air in New York City; it is broadcast nationwide starting the following year.

1954 From April to June, the Army-McCarthy Senate hearings have Americans glued to their sets; *Disneyland* debuts on ABC in October.

1955 *Gunsmoke*, one of the first adult westerns, debuts on CBS in September; another adult Western, *Cheyenne*, debuts the same month and becomes the first of many successful series from Warner Brothers.

1957 Jack Paar becomes host of *The Tonight Show*.

1959 NBC's western *Bonanza* becomes the first prime-time network series to be filmed in color.

1960 On September 26, the first of four televised debates takes place between presidential candidates John F. Kennedy and Richard Nixon; Kennedy, the "television president," is elected in November.

1961 In a landmark speech, FCC chairman Newton Minow declares television "a vast wasteland."

1962 On September 26, *The Beverly Hillbillies* debuts on CBS and becomes the top rated show; on October 22, President Kennedy reports on the Cuban Missile Crisis on a live television broadcast.

1963 Kennedy is assassinated on November 22, and the networks suspend all other programming for an unprecedented four days.

1964 The British rock group the Beatles makes their first live appearance on American television on *The Ed Sullivan Show* in February; an act of Congress requires that all new television sets be capable of receiving ultrahigh frequency (UHF) stations.

1965 The escalation of the Vietnam War brings intense television coverage of a war for the first time in history.

1967 On August 27 the final episode of ABC's dramatic series *The Fugitive* becomes the most watched single program of the decade; the Public Broadcasting Act establishes the Public Broadcasting System (PBS).

1968 In February, CBS anchorman Walter Cronkite publicly criticizes the handling of the Vietnam War in a news special; President Lyndon Johnson announces a month later than he will not run for re-election.

1969 On July 20, the *Apollo 11* moon landing is broadcast live.

1970 *The Mary Tyler Moore Show* debuts on CBS.

1971 *All in the Family* debuts on CBS.

1972 Home Box Office (HBO), the first premier cable channel, is launched; *M*A*S*H,* a unique wartime sitcom, premieres on CBS.

1975 *Saturday Night Live,* a late night weekend comedy show, debuts on NBC.

1976 Ted Turner beams his Atlanta, Georgia, station TBS to a satellite, making it the first "superstation."

1977 *Roots,* a groundbreaking miniseries about African-American history, runs for eight consecutive nights in January.

1979 The Japanese produce the first high-definition television (HDTV) system.

1980 Ted Turner launches Cable News Network (CNN), the first twenty-four-hour, all-news network.

1981 *Hill Street Blues,* an innovative police drama, debuts on NBC.

1984 *The Cosby Show,* one of the most popular shows of the decade, debuts on NBC.

1987 The Fox Network, a fourth commercial network, is launched.

1988 *Cops,* one of the first examples of reality television, debuts on Fox.

1989 *The Simpsons,* the longest-running sitcom and animated show on television, debuts on Fox.

1992 On May 22, Johnny Carson hosts *The Tonight Show* for the last time.

1993 Cable television provides its customers with Internet service for the first time.

1998 The televised launching of the space shuttle *Discovery* in November is the first public HDTV broadcast on American television.

1999 *The Sopranos*, the most popular show in cable history, debuts on HBO; President Bill Clinton signs the Satellite Home Viewer Improvement Act (SHVIA).

2005 Five million viewers watch American Online's (AOL's) live Webcast of the Live 8 Concert series.

Web Sites

The Encyclopedia of Television
http://www.museum.tv/archives/etv./index.html.

History of Technology
http://www.fcc.gov/omd/history/TV

History of Television
http://histv2.free.fr/cadrehistory.htm

Television History—The First Seventy-five Years
http://www.tvhistory.tv/

Television History—The History of TV
http://inventors.about.com/library/inventors/bltelvision.htm

Television Shows and Series
http://www.tvparty.com
http://www.tcacres.com

Books

FOR STUDENTS

Berry, Joy. *Every Kid's Guide to Watching Television Intelligently.* Danbury, CT: Children's Press, 1987.

Calabro, Marion. *Zap! A Brief History of Television.* New York: Four Winds Press, 1992.

Teitelbaum, Michael. *Radio and Television* Great Inventions series. Milwaukee, WI: World Almanac Library, 2005.

FOR TEACHERS

Fireman, Judy. *TV Book: The Ultimate Television Book.* New York: Workman Publishing, 1977.

Garner, Joe. *Stay Tuned: Television's Unforgettable Moments.* Kansas City, MO: Andrews McMeel Publishers, 2002.

Goldstein, Norm. *The History of Television.* New York: Portland House, 1991.

Kisseloff, Jeff. *The Box: An Oral History of Television 1920–1961.* New York: Penguin, 1995.

O'Neil, Thomas. *The Emmys: Star Wars, Showdowns, and the Supreme Test of TV's Best.* New York: Penguin, 1992.

Stark, Steven D. *Glued to the Set: The 60 Television Shows and Events That Made Us Who We Are Today.* New York: Dell, 1997.

Index

Page numbers for illustrations are in **boldface**.

About the Author

Steven Otfinoski has written more than 120 books for young readers. His many biographies include books about Jesse Jackson, Oprah Winfrey, John Wilkes Booth, Nelson Mandela, and Boris Yeltsin. He has also written books on geography, world history, rock music, public speaking, and writing.

He is the author of *Marco Polo: To China and Back, Francisco Coronado: In Search of the Seven Cities of Gold, Vasco Nuñez de Balboa: Discoverer of the Pacific, Juan Ponce de León: Discoverer of Florida,* and *Henry Hudson: In Search of the Northwest Passage* in the Great Explorations series. His other works for Marshall Cavendish include the twelve-volume transportation series for early readers Here We Go! and books on New Hampshire, Georgia, Maryland, and Washington State in the Celebrate the States and It's My State! series.

Two of his books, *Triumph and Terror: The French Revolution* and *Poland: Nation in Transitions,* were chosen as Books for the Teen Age by the New York Public Library.

Otfinoski is also a produced playwright and has his own theater company History Alive! that brings plays about American history to schoolchildren. He lives with his wife, Beverly, and their two children in Connecticut.